FROM THE LIBRARY OF

WILLIAM THOMPSON

MORE STORIES
OF THE
OLD DUCK HUNTERS

MORE STORIES
OF THE
OLD DUCK HUNTERS

GORDON MacQUARRIE

COMPILED & EDITED BY ZACK TAYLOR

Drawings by Paul Birling
from photographs originally appearing with Gordon MacQuarrie stories
published in Field & Stream and Sports Afield

WILLOW CREEK PRESS • OSHKOSH, WISCONSIN

Published in 1983 by Willow Creek Press, P.O. Box 2266, Oshkosh, WI 54903.

ISBN 0-932558-18-6
Printed in the U.S.A.

As solemnly as possible given the circumstances, this book is dedicated to all bonafide, God fearing, paid-in-full members of the Old Duck Hunter's Association, Incorrigible . . . no matter what.

Forward

When I decided many years ago to compile the first group of MacQuarrie stories, it was my plan to leaf through the old outdoor magazines (the New York Public Library had them all) to discover and copy them. This would have been a tedious task and an expensive one. Copying then cost 25 cents a page, as much as the issues themselves at the time. Happily I found that Mac's widow and his daughter had saved his manuscripts and kindly sent them to me.

Somehow I instinctively knew there would be a pattern to the stories, a story behind the stories. Indeed there was a memorable one. First came the rollicking friendship deepening to love, the death of Mr. President, followed by the story of MacQuarrie going it alone in the cabin and in a situation hardly equalled in pathos telling how good it was. Finally MacQuarrie finds a new Mr. President and the stories start anew...only to be shut off by the author's untimely death.

This untold story is that I had a hand in some of this. I came to Sports Afield in 1955 and one of the first things I suggested to then-editor, Ted Kesting, was that I write MacQuarrie and ask him for more of Mr. President stories. Ted readily agreed. I made the request and the series flowed again. What I realized only years later is that when Al Peck, MacQuarrie's father-in-law and the model for Mr. President, died the writer had no thought to continue on. Mr. President was dead, how could there be any more Old Duck Hunters' Association, Inc. stories? My letter was an invitation no professional writer could resist. It came as the spur for Mac-

Quarrie to find another companion. The MacQuarrie talent easily elevated him to the Presidency.

There will be no play within a play in these pages. We will take the yarns as they came out of the redhead's typewriter. (Unlike the first book where I received typewritten manuscript all these stories appeared in publication and can be roughly dated from that.) We can watch his themes and moods develop. You can see him sharpen as a writer. Most of all, look for what we who have worked on the books have come to call the "MacQuarrie Magic." It starts out small, a touch here and there. Slowly it grows until whole passages are poetic, bursting with description and color. The humor, too, is hesitant and shaky at first. Not for long. Smiles turn into chuckles. And, to top it off, tell me if the man spinning these yarns isn't having more doggone fun than anybody.

Contents

Introduction

This book, like the first compilation, is a labor of love. Correction: A labor of many loves. The first is mine. My debt to MacQuarrie is deep and real. As a boy I read each story eagerly as it appeared. Naturally they shaped my attitude toward the outdoors. (And I'm not much of a trout fisherman.) But they went far beyond that. They helped teach me what life is all about. Friendship. Decency. Fun. Feeling deeply. Savoring. Good stuff like that. When I was appointed Boats Editor and had time, my first thought was to repay the debt. That may sound self-serving but it is the truth.

Secondly there have been the loves of his widow, Ellen MacQuarrie Wilson, a resident of York, England, herself an author, and his daughter, Mrs. Sally Wiemer of California. Their attitude, one with which I heartily concur, can be summed up by a statement of Mrs. Wilson's. "I am of the school that would print all (the stories), as even Gordon's weaker work was better than most things I read!" Their cooperation has been total.

In the intervening years since ODHA came out, many have written me asking where more ODHA stories could be found. I could only direct them to old issues of the magazines. I did so to a John Case in 1977. A Minneapolis resident, he found Field and Streams and Sports Afields dating from 1930 to 1950 at the Agricultural campus of the University of Minnesota. He copied 29 of them in book form and sent me a copy!

I was stunned. But like any member schooled in the ODHA tradition I rose to the occasion. I picked up the phone and called Tom Petrie of the

Willow Creek Press, publisher of the present paperback edition. I told him what I held in my hands and asked if he wanted to publish another group of the incomparable yarns. "Heck yes," said Tom. In fact he may have said, "Hell, yes."

When my father died and we sold his house I found nine old editions of Field and Stream saved from the 1945-1946 period when I was in the army. These contributed several more stories that John's search had missed including, thankfully, Nervous Breakdown. Mrs. Wiemer kindly sent me copies of the original manuscripts which yielded a few more. They also revealed another labor of love. Editors love to tinker with writers' copy. A comparison of the originals with what appeared in print showed that with MacQuarrie "hands off" was the rule.

I have saved the best for last. There are twenty stories as yet unpublished. Some great ones. Man Tired, When The White Throats Sing, The Bluebills Died at Dawn. If this edition meets with approval, it is our plan to publish those. In that regard I ask anyone who runs across an ODHA story to so advise me by sending the title. I have no doubt there are more.

There are three authors from the same era whose works are still in print — Gordon MacQuarrie, Havilah Babcock and Nash Buckingham. It is of immense satisfaction to me that I had a part in adding MacQuarrie's name to that list.

Zack Taylor
Canvasback Lane
Easton, MD

This is the first of this series published in Field and Stream in January of 1932. It is fitting that to start it is about a slamaroo of a duck shooting day. In Ducks? You Bat You! *that appeared in the first collection we saw MacQuarrie's introduction to the sport. But here he is an old hand, sharp of eye to kill 15 birds with 22 shells and make a story out of it.*

It might be added to save the reader the trouble of figuring it out that the frequent allusions to automobiles, new and (mostly) used, occur because Mr. President owned a car agency in Duluth.

Bluebill Day

I know where three lakes of north Wisconsin blue challenge the monotonous march of jack-pine and scrub-oak over the left-hand corner of the state. The lakes of which I speak are a triumvirate among thousands of similar bodies whose shores have been inhospitable to the settler and benevolent to the angler and the hunter. These lakes seem to have several names, but most of the people thereabout call them the Richards Lakes. Less than two hundred yards separates one from the other. They stretch east and west. The one farthest east is the largest, nearly a mile long and half as wide. The one farthest west is not quite so large. The one in the center of the chain is the smallest but deepest. From its northern shore projects a stocky headland that narrows to a slim point, clad with trees to within fifty feet of the tip. One dazzling, warm October day I shot ducks on this point. In the center of four trees, grouped in a perfect square, I sat on a shell-box and enjoyed the easiest duck shooting I ever expect to encounter outside of a rich man's club.

At noon of that memorable day, Joe dropped into the headquarters of the Old Duck Hunters' Association. Out-of-doors the bright October sun flooded the flaming oaks and pines with the warmth of August. The lake, on the shores of which headquarters are established, seemed drinking in the unseasonal heat wave, as though to fortify itself against approaching winter. Only that morning we had hunted, with indifferent shooting, on a near-by slough. The President of the Association was taking forty winks

to make up for the early beginning of the day.

"Let's get going to Richards Lakes," cried Joe of the stentorian voice and boundless energy.

"Not today, thanks," was the President's dictum.

"Weather's a bit too fine, isn't it, Joe?" I asked, wiping my brow. I was warm, and the fever of Indian summer made me so lazy that I had not taken the trouble to doff heavy garments.

"Told you yesterday we were going to Richards Lakes," said Joe. "There is always good duck shooting over there. Got the boat on the trailer, decoys in the car, and we're all set."

"Mr. President," I interposed, "it is apparent that the Honorable Joe took our promises of yesterday in good faith. If it is in order, I suggest that we accompany him to the fabled lakes and find out if all he says is true. Take your casting rod along and see if there are any bass over there."

The President is a lover of variety. Duck hunting he adores, and bass fishing he worships. Surfeited with the former, my appeal found its mark.

"Over-ruled," he moaned, and while he gloatd over the joys of fishing in a new and comparatively unfished lake I pondered on the useful purpose the rod might serve in the retrieving of a dead duck, caught offshore in the weeds.

Ten miles of journeying over a winding, up-and-down, sand trail brought us to the westernmost lake. It gleamed brightly through the trees, but there was not a duck in sight on its surface. On to the second we drove.

"The farthest one is usually the best," opined Joe.

"I'll take this one," I volunteered, "if no one else wants it."

The personnel of the Association agreed. I was transported across the lake and given half the decoys, then Joe and the President departed with the boat for the conquest of the farthest lake. My blind, I discovered, had been thoughtfully made for me some fifteen years before, when four spruce cones fell so as to form the corners of a tree square six feet on all sides. I heard the jolting car and trailer disappear on the road to the other lake, and sat on the shore for a moment's contemplation of autumn's glory.

The decoys bobbed slightly in the wind, which was blowing directly off the point. The sun glanced ridiculously off their painted forms. They seemed utterly impotent to attract ducks. Indeed, there was not a duck in sight anywhere, on the lake or in the air. I made a pillow of my heavy blanket coat and lay on my back, staring upward at a peaceful blue sky that seemed never to have looked down upon the flight of ducks. On such a day, I speculated, ducks would likely be resting undisturbed in the hundreds of inaccessible pot-holes that cover the region.

I was jolted from my day-dreams by a tremendous sound like thin silk being torn — that billowing whisper which filled the air when ducks are flying *en masse.* It seemed incredible, but when I raised my head I was staggered at what I saw. A thousand — maybe two thousand — ducks were in the air. I knew they must have come from the lake to the east of me and had doubtless been frightened into flight at the approach of the other two hunters. They came up from behind the trees on the high ridge that separates the two lakes. Obviously my lake was their chosen objective, and there was I, lying like a ninny behind the decoys, day-dreaming, my sheathed double gun and shell-box reposing in the tree blind fifty feet in back of me!

I remained motionless as the main flight passed over in fairly close range. Then, not thirty yards from me, a flock of forty or fifty plowed into the water. There was nothing else for me to do but dig out for the blind, and as I did so the visitors roared away to join the throng of ever-increasing friends that had swept to a landing at the upper end of the lake.

With trembling fingers I assembled the gun and fumbled in the shell-box. Thunderation! There was only a part of a box of shells — twenty-two by actual count. I felt like walking down the shore and making a general announcement to the ducks that they might all go now, because I was going home to soak my head in a water barrel. How many times had I toted that preposterous shell-box in rain and shine, filled to the muzzle with no less than eight boxes of shells, only to find opportunity for one or two shots?

Ducks were scooting across my point like dandelion bloom before the wind. At the far end of my lake their brethren and sisters were "per-r-r-utting" and quacking in bluebill and mallard sociability. Later I learned that there was only one flock of mallards among the hundreds of black-hooded bluebills, and they tarried not long. I deliberately let flock after flock dust across the point while I thought out a plan of action.

With twenty-two shells, it would take some powerful lucky shooting to bag the limit of fifteen ducks; so I decided to take only the easy ones. The wind was in my favor. If they decoyed as the others had, there was one —

[16]

and only one — opening in the blind from which to shoot. It was a perfect port-hole frame with spruce boughs. A shot from any other angle, without considerable re-arranging of my blind, or the building of an entirely new one, was impossible and blind building was not in my thoughts.

I would have to be careful, but maybe I could make my twenty-two shells do the trick. My principal fear in not doing proper honor to my membership in the Old Duck Hunters' Association lay in the tongue-lashing the President would administer when he learned of my plight. He had often cautioned me to be ready for any emergency; in fact, it was at his urging that I had often lugged pounds and pounds of shells to remote sloughs and duck passes without any immediate recompense.

Off to my left, on the other lake, I heard the first boom of guns. My companions were all set in a blind somewhere, I conjectured, and would likely drive more ducks to me. Sure enough! A flock of butterballs topped the ridge between the two lakes and slanted straight for my decoys. It was a murderously easy shot, and the two birds dropped stone-dead. Two ducks and twenty shells left. I had to get thirteen more with twenty shells! For me, that is impossible under normal conditions. There must be no silly shots at high or fast-flying ducks, lest I wound one, and then, liver-heart that I am, I would probably waste four or five shells putting it out of misery. No, I decided, I must take only the easy ones, and take them permanently.

The offshore wind quickly wafted my dead pair out into the lake. They would be picked up later on the opposite shore, exactly at the place where the returning lodge members, now at lake number three, would park the car preparatory to coming after me in the boat.

Suddenly there were eight mallards, high overhead, coming straight across the point. Evidently they had parted company with the sputtering bluebills. It was a shot I could not resist. I leaped from the blinding blind and shot, from a miserable stance, at the first of the octette. The third came down with a sensational somersaulting and was soon bobbing with the wind toward the opposite shore. I occupied the interim before the next flock came, with mathematics. Nineteen shells left and three ducks dead. Not bad. If my arithmetic held out, I might make a score.

My eye accidentally caught a movement on the water through the hindering spruce growth. I adjusted my vision to a new and larger opening, and was astounded to find every one of my bluebills swimming eagerly toward me, the front-rank leaders not one hundred yards distant!

They came right along, and I decided that such foolery had to stop. With my gun to my shoulder, I shouted at them and the afternoon call broke up in wild confusion. I fired both barrels and even tried to reload for a second chance before looking around for the dead and wounded. Search as I would, I could find nary a feather on the water! The legion of ducks had come and gone, offering me the kind of a shot any greenhorn could have scored on. My shame was numbing. A handful of incomers flirted low over the decoys an instant later, and I was so flustered that I made two perfect misses.

Ordinarily duck hunters with any pride whatsoever draw the well-known veil over such happenings. It is much easier to forget and ask forgiveness of oneself, before one develops an inferiority complex and loses all confidence. Such experiences prove strongly the influence of mental attitude in duck shooting. One miss leads to another, and that is largely due to the inability of the hunter to readjust himself mentally to his usual form.

Fifteen shells left and twelve ducks to go. Things looked bad. The bogey of wounded ducks was to be considered. I waste no time in dispatching them. I have even carried heavy shot in my shell-box, for their long range, to reach the wounded ones that drop quite a ways out. Until you have tried it you have no idea of the number of shells that can be wasted in trying to stop a wounded duck.

From the other lake I heard intermittent shooting and concluded that the bass had been forgotten. The shots were usually followed by a movement of ducks. We were driving the birds back and forth between us, although some of them darted westward over the hill and sought refuge in lake number one, where there was no one to disturb them. My three dead ducks were, by this time, out of sight in the wavelets, on the other side of the lake.

The next opportunity took the form of a squadron of bluebills, coming dead on. The white markings on the heads of the females were plainly discernible when I fired. Two dropped with the first shot. They flared to the right, and the second shot, the only genuine one I made that day, caught the last duck far out. To make it I once more scrambled out of the tree fortress and fired. It restored my confidence to see that duck take a hard, slanting fall to the water, completely dead. But one of the other pair was wabbling his head! I took no chances with him, but advanced to the water's edge and executed him instantly. Three ducks with three shots —

I was keeping up fairly well.

Nine ducks to go and twelve shells left. What wouldn't I have given for a case of shells, so that I might accept this shooting in true sporting fashion, taking them as they came?

Most of my attention was occupied with watching through the natural porthole of the blind, so that I was taken completely by surprise when another flock of birds swam into the decoys, this time from the left. I was about to raise them and try a shot when I caught another shadowy movement through the spruce. Not fifteen feet from me, close inshore, swam thirty or forty bluebills and ringnecks, headed for the decoys! And swimming!

I wondered if these ducks had suddenly gone crazy. Perhaps they had eaten of some lotus-like weed from the depths of the Richards Lakes. Or — and this is more likely — they were newcomers in the country, fresh from some wild haunt to the north where the destroying hand of man was unknown. I let them swim away from me, toward the decoys, and planned a campaign.

My other shots on departing ducks, I figured, must have been failures because of undershooting. This time I struggled from the trees as quickly as the encumbering branches would permit, and caught the rising ducks from a better position. To stop these ducks one must swing and raise the gun simultaneously. On teal and mallards rising suddenly, it is mostly a vertical movement of the gun barrel, but the bluebills and many other varieties possess no power of leaping straight into the air. Their take-off is more like that of an airplane. They have yet to master the trick of going straight — or nearly straight — up in the air.

The first shot missed. The second found a fair mark, and the duck, which I judged to be a ringneck, dropped dead.

Eight ducks to go and ten shells left. The ducks were gaining on me! I must do some more merciless shooting through the porthole at incomers with outstretched wings, ready to alight. The next chance materialized in that way, and two remained behind out of a flock of a dozen or more. Six ducks to go and eight shells left. All this time ducks were coursing across my point in the blazing sun from every angle. A persistent bombardment echoed from the other lake.

To have shot on this point from a blind of conventional build, with an unlimited supply of shells, would have been nothing short of duck murder. There would have been many misses, but who cares? It would have afforded an afternoon's lesson in point shooting from every angle that I have never had and, what's more, that I need badly. Another straight-out chance at incomers ready to light netted three, all dead with only two shots. I waited for those three with malice aforethought, and they died suddenly and satisfactorily. That left three ducks still to be downed and six shells with which to do it.

A pot-shot offered itself when four foolishly swam in, but I passed it up. Not only is it a bit rough to take them in this manner, but they are, be assured, hard to kill on the water. Many a greedy hunter can testify to that. I let them swim off. When a small flock flew in shortly after, to leave two of their number dead behind, the swimmers arose fussily fifty yards away and departed.

Only one more duck to go now and four loaded shells! I was doing famously. Surely I could afford to gamble with those four shells. I abandoned the tormenting blind and stood motionless on the end of the point. My presence did not seem to frighten the moving flocks. A large bunch from the other lake came over high, and two of the precious shells were gone, to no purpose. This flock was followed by a single, coming high from the left. The first one missed, the second sent him plunging down, and my shooting was over.

I sat on the point as motionless as I could, and witnessed one of the most amazing duck shows I have ever heard of in this part of the country. There were hundreds in the air from time to time, and two large bunches swam into the decoys, oblivious of my presence in the open. They seemed to realize that all was not well, for they approached slowly and tarried but a short time before paddling away. When I retreated to the blind later and was completely hidden, several small bunches swam into the decoys, looked them over and departed hastily.

Then the car, with jolting trailer, creaked along the sand trail across the lake. It was growing dim by that time, and soon I made out Joe's lights through the trees. Laughter drifted across the water to me as they unloaded the boat. It sounded as though they were feeling sorry for me, left to my own devices on that point, while they had chosen the other lake where the shooting was supposed to be better. The President came over for me in the boat.

"Gee, I'm sorry you weren't with us," he began. "All the ducks in upper Wisconsin had a grand reunion right under our noses."

"Don't feel sorry for me, your honor," I replied. "My fifteen ducks are over against the shore, and if I were any kind of a sport I would have killed them all with a slingshot!"

MacQuarrie and the Brule. There's a marriage made in heaven. He loved the stream and returned to it again and again in his writings. As the title suggests Upstream — Downstream *is really two different stories. The first is MacQuarrie fishing alone with dry flies, taking three nice fish. It has much the same flavor as Hemingway's much-published* Big Two Hearted River, *a man alone, each strike carefully drawn, each fight described in detail.*

The second story relinquishes the smokey poetry in favor of buffoonery. Hizzoner pits himself against a fishless pool, then against a mighty fish that comes out of it. At a climax of the fight, MacQuarrie slips and goes into the water. It was probably not the first time one or the other of this duo would go overboard and will certainly not be the last. It is one of the writer's favorite ploys.

Upstream Downstream

"I will not go upstream and fish that gin-clear water with a spinner on the first day of any season!" It was Al himself, more or less famous president of the Old Duck Hunters, Inc., speaking, alias Rainbow Al from May 1 to September 1.

"You'd rather sling spinners in the soup down near Lake Superior, then?" I asked.

"My boy," quoth the sage of the North Country, "there are two ways to fish the Brule River in the early season. One is with flies up above, where it's clear; the other is with spinners down below, where it's discolored. The first way you get nothing but a sore wrist from casting. The second way you hook at least one great big fish that may smash your tackle and break your heart. If it's a big rainbow, it's a red-letter day. If it's a big steelhead, it's a red-letter day and you get a stiff wrist to boot."

"Your Honor," said I sorrowfully, "you are a sinful and wanton fish hog. For several years now you have eschewed the plebian spinner and worms in favor of the aristocratic dry fly in all seasons, and here you are, backsliding like any regenerate after a revival. Where is your sense of decency?"

"The call of the big guy is too strong," replied Al. "I long to spin a spinner in the dark waters of McNeil's pool."

"But think of the fun upstream with flies — especially dry flies."

"Yes, it might be more fun," he admitted reluctantly.

I saw that he was weakening, and pressed on with my best argument —

an invitation to visit a friend who had a special road of his own leading into the upstream waters of the 66-mile river. So we went upstream, but I could see, as we climbed into waders, that he was pessimistic.

Ice still lingered around some cedar tree roots as we invaded the dank river valley. Not very encouraging for a fly-fisherman who had hoped for months to try out some new flies and some new, very light opaque leaders. Heavy waders and extra socks inside gave a welcome warmth — until we stepped into the river!

We separated, each to pursue his opening-day luck in the moving flood of ice water. The veteran strode off with resolute steps for some special places downstream, while I waded through a stretch of mud bottom to the current-washed stones of midstream, intending to work upward with dry flies for a while at least.

The shadows on the Brule were pretty long, but the sun was bright behind the cedars, giving promise of warmth later on. Someone ought to invent waders with fur-lined pockets for early-season fishing. There just isn't any place where one may take the chill out of numbed fingers, unless he folds his arms over his breast and tucks his digits into his armpits — and a fellow must hang on to his rod. The cold penetrated to the marrow, through waders, heavy socks and mackinaw pants. Every so often I was compelled to get out of the water and perch on a rock in Napoleonic pose until circulation was restored sufficiently to permit another go at it.

For a good two hours I fished a 50-yard stretch that invariably produces good browns and rainbows, and not only saw no rises but did not see a sign of a fish in the water. The lingering chill of winter seemed to have laid a killing hand upon the stream, although I knew there should be lots of Lake Superior run rainbows lying in every pool. Search as I would, I could see no sign of any insect life on the water. If the fish saw the Brown Bivisible, plain Coachman and Badger Bivisible that I laid down over them, they gave no sign. I worked with the carefulness of the conscientious early-season practitioner — the way one can apply himself to the tediousness of form is remarkable for the first few trips of the season. But the fish responded not.

When I reached the head of the pool, I retraced my steps and after waiting several minutes again fished upstream with a favorite of mine — a small wet Royal Coachman, well dunked before beginning, and fished as deep as I could get it to go.

But nothing happened, which may be a poor way to start a fishing story but adheres quite strictly to the facts. I did take courage, however, for I am one of those superstitious anglers who feels that the day starts auspiciously when everything doesn't happen all at once. Several river canoes passed me, headed downstream, and I pitied the passengers. Most of them were purple-lipped and shivering as they sat in their boats carried along by the current. One boat came along bearing two anglers who usually take fish, and they told me they had not even seen a fish rise since they started at 4:00 A.M. I felt licked. When those two gentlemen don't get them, not many others do. But it's always darkest just before the dawn.

It was getting warmer. The sun was flooding the valley; and although the lower half of me was congealed, I could take comfort in the upper half being fairly warm. I quit the stream and took to the woods, aiming for a popular spot where the river is divided by an island and the two chutes come together in a fast flow of water. Scores of rainbows had been spawning here a few weeks before. A friend occupied the head of the pool and was going good with a Colorado spinner and angleworms. He had three rainbows. I left him and continued upstream, through the difficult timber that flanks both sides of the Brule. There's one nice thing about that path of the river — there are no paths worn by anglers, which is in its favor.

The sun had me pretty well thawed out the next time I launched myself into the river, at the lower end of a slow stretch, the head of which is a famous pool. Out over the tail of the pool went the Brown Bivisible, time and again, with no results. Fishermen passing me in canoes occasionally expressed amazement that I should be trying dry flies. I will never forget the satisfaction I experienced when one of them saw my fly sailing by, attached to that new opaque leader. He could not see the leader and asked me if I had not snapped off the fly. If a man could not see it, perhaps a fish could not, either.

I gradually worked up until I was casting over water that must have been five feet deep. When a leader that you had hoped would prove invisible is actually invisible to an old trout hawk, it tends to buoy you up. With more faith in myself and my outfit, I worked the bivisible persistently, carefully, time after time, until my arm ached, and that's hard work if one has neither seen a fish rise or leap. The Brown Bivisible, incidentally, appeals to me as a good fly to use when in doubt — or any other time. There is nothing in insect life like it, but the white twist of hackle dancing over the water enables the angler to see it better.

At that, I believe it would not have been necessary to watch the fly

[25]

closely in order to hook the fish that finally did rise to it. It was a heavy brown, and never was there a more deliberate, confident attack upon a fly. The fish seemed to have been lying directly beneath it and took it with very little commotion on the surface.

When he felt the line, he dived into the deepest water of the hole, running into the current to do it. A heavy windstorm of last summer had blown a cedar tree into the hole. Part of the tree was still green, its roots clinging tenaciously to the soil, but I knew that a lot of tree was under water right where Mr. Brown was headed for. I put on all the pressure that I dared, and he came out — came out strong, going downstream. He made one glistening leap during which I saw his every spot and then nosed into the bottom in a series of powerful jerks. After that he was mine. I let him play dog in the shallower water, halted a few desperate attempts to get back into the hole with the tree in it, and finally netted him. He measured eighteen inches.

Then I forgot about the cold water entirely! Here were fish that would rise to a fly! Here was opportunity, pleasure, thrill — sport. How glad I was that I had persuaded the honorable Mr. Al to come upstream with me!

Now things were different. Every cast found me looking forward to a rise. Now every inch of the water seemed to give promise of a fish. So does the first fish of the season establish within one that most uncertain of fishermen's foibles — faith — without which no fish are caught and no fun is had.

After a rest of about fifteen minutes, I had begun to retrieve my cast when the second fish shot out from beneath the submerged cedar trees and struck where the fly had been. I saw him as he lifted surfaceward, and my heart beat fast. I know now that I should have waited, but I could not. A few false casts, and the bivisible settled down in the center of the rippling circles where the trout had broken water. My fish had not gone home after the first try. But he started for home the minute he seized the fly, on the next try, and once more I risked the light leader to keep him out of the drowned tree.

I think I had right there as good an opportunity as I ever had to compare the fighting qualities of the brown and the native brook trout. And the native wins over the brown. Attribute it to the colder water if you will, with the explanation that the brookie was more at home there, but this does not satisfy me. The brown was a bigger fish, I learned eventually.

The native proved to be about two inches shorter than the brown; and while he remained under water and fought the dogged, persistent fight of the typical brook trout, it must be recorded the fight was a good one. I did not catch a glimpse of him until he was netted. It is not often nowadays that one can stretch out a fat, 16-inch native squaretail on a rock.

Back at it again I went. It was getting along toward noon, and the occasional canoes passing me headed downstream contained more cheerful passengers. Up in Durant's channel a man had taken two rainbows. In the rips above Cedar Island another had used a fly effectively on eight nice browns and rainbows, and all along the stream the first-day fiends were reporting things as looking up, with fish rising and a hatch of something or other appearing. More confident than ever, I returned to the fray with a new Brown Bivisible. How I came to love that fly!

I moved around to a glassy slide where the water emptied into the pool. The current here was not fast but much faster than that in the pool, and the work of casting and handling was, therefore, faster and more tiring. I stood so that the fly would alight about twenty feet above where the sharp break of the water occurred and let the fly slide down into the slower water. Faith was bolstered now with past experience, as I knew fish usually lay there, especially toward evening. And it was shallow enough so that a fish would not have to strain his eyesight upward to catch sight of the fly.

The third trout was on and away down the slide, into the pool, before I realized what was happening. He must have known about the drowned cedar tree — but so did I. The leader held him from wrecking me in the tree; so he continued on downstream, and I scrambled after as well as I could, shipping only a little water as I skirted the edge of the pool in record time. He got out of the slower water into faster water, however, and lay broadside to the current, the better to fight the hated line that held him.

I would not have been too sorry if he had beaten me just then, but when I finally netted him I was doubly glad — he was another native just about like the first. Later on he and his kind will have abandoned that part of the stream entirely for the colder holes in the impenetrable swamps far upstream, where in some places the sun's rays never touch the water directly.

I gloated. Two big natives and a brown the first day — and they were just starting to hit dry flies. It was after lunch time, and I returned

[27]

through the tangled woods to the starting point. In a pool fifty yards below the appointed rendezvous was Al, up to his hips in the stream and working like a nailer, with the sourest expression imaginable on his face. I hardly had the courage to tell him of my luck, but when I did he came snorting out of the river like a disgusted hippo, took down his rod, stowed away his gear and set out for the car.

"Boy," he stated finally, "you and I are going downstream for meat. That is, I'm going downstream. Are you? It's my car, you know."

"But they're hitting dry flies here now. It's warming up."

"They're hitting no dry flies of mine," retaliated the enraged angler. "If I'm going to catch up with those three you have, I've got to make big medicine with a spinner and angleworms. And mark you, all I want is just one chance. Never shall it be said of me that I got licked on the Brule or any other stream because I was too high-hat to use bait."

A fellow can do nothing with a man like that. He got his chance. My anticipation of a glorious afternoon with flies turned to dreary consideration of how far a rainbow can see when the water is as brown as it gets down at McNeil's pool so early in the season. It was not a pleasant drive for me in one sense, for the light of battle was kindled in Al's eye and any mention of my three fish brought prodigious snuffing and snorting and belligerent promises of what he'd do when he got where he wanted to go! The honorable Al can be ornery without actually offending. And he doesn't get licked easily.

"But you're licked today," I badgered him when he pulled up beside the big lone spruce in McNeil's meadow and saw the brown flood of the Brule sweeping by.

"A fish can't even see a spinner in that water," I protested.

"It works both ways, son," retorted the confirmed optimist. "A fish can't see me, either."

In we went, drifting downstream with the current and letting spinners sweep across it before retrieving them. Spring fishing for steelheads and rainbows is the closest thing to salmon fishing that this country affords. The big rainbows from Lake Superior, which begin coming up as soon as the ice-choked mouth of the river is opened, have done as much as anything to make the river famous over the world. Rainbows of ten pounds are not uncommon. Several over twenty pounds in weight have been taken, and the hide of one monster reputed to weigh over twenty-five pounds is tacked on the wall of a restaurant in the town of Brule.

[29]

I was leading the way in the battle of spinners, and I placed my greatest confidence in a long, deep pool about two hundred yards below our starting place — called McNeil's pool by many fishermen. At this part of the river one is not more than three or four miles by river from Lake Superior, and big fish are likely to be caught there the year around. One rainbow about a foot long hit my spinner and shook it free in the first leap. But no matter. There was a pool; and glory be, when I rounded the bend in the river, no one was in it, which was unusual for the opening day.

I worked over the pool for about a half hour before Mr. President caught up with me.

"There's not a fish in it," I remarked. I was mad, of course, at the thought of missing the upstream fishing.

"If there's no fish in that pool, there's no fish in the Brule," he answered. "Therefore, your allegation is a patent falsehood, made with malicious and malevolent intent to destroy the morale of your boon companion."

He doubled up his leader for greater strength, casting funny little glances toward me. I climbed out and sat on the bank in the sun, leaving him to his bitter task. I dislike fishing in murky water, but the faith of my companion is far greater than mine. Maybe that's why he usually catches more fish.

I grew weary of watching his arm go back and then forward to send the spinner searching into every corner of the pool. I lay on my back, shielding my eyes from the sun with my hat, a picture of piscatorial contentment. It was getting on toward four o'clock.

I heard a solid plop, like a log being dropped into the water, which was followed by an involuntary groan from Al. It caused me to sit up. Across the sun-dappled pool I saw him pull his hat down a little more snugly and advance into deeper water. He just looked at me as though he would gladly break my neck for just sitting there and doing nothing. His stubborn lip became more stubborn, if that is possible, and he finally mumbled, "No fish in this pool, eh?"

"Was that a fish that rose?" I asked.

"It was not a fish," he snapped. "It was a crocodile, and it didn't rise, either. It just lifted itself out of the water on its elbows, saw me, and fell back in terror!"

"I hope he bites your leg off."

He declined to answer, but continued the wearying game of shooting his spinner out, letting it ride, then retrieving. The monotony of the thing

[30]

was maddening. I watched him change from spinner and worms to plain spinner, then plain worms, then salmon eggs and spinner, then — so help me! — spinner with salmon eggs and worms all together. Then he went ashore and dug into his war bag for some little plugs, which he tossed around for what seemed an hour. Finally he let the worms drag on the bottom until he caught a sucker and used a part of the sucker's belly for bait. When that didn't work, he dug still farther into his resources and produced an assortment of bucktail spinners and unnamed creations that were intended originally for bass and pike. By that time he was talking to himself, and I was actually beginning to feel sorry for him. But of such stuff are great fishermen made.

After a while I began feeling sorry for myself. I wanted to get home that day. The conviction began to grow on me that he would never go if he didn't hook the fish. I resumed my siesta on the bank. Something told me he was going to catch the darned fish. He usually did, and I was beginning to feel a little bit licked myself, maybe. I counted about twenty-five of the soft splashes made by his lures as they hit the pool's surface. Then I slept.

"He's on!"

It was a pleasant way to be awakened. I leaped to my feet and began running up and down the bank like an excited retriever. Al's rod was whipping furiously. One jump took the fish — a huge steelhead — about four feet out of water.

There are those who say brother steelhead and brother rainbow are one and the same fish in fighting ability, and there are many who claim that they are the same fish with different coloration. I have never counted the number of scales along their lateral lines. I have never compared their back-bones for a count of vertebrae I will admit, further, that I can't always tell them apart, but I do know this — that our friend in the pool was a steelhead and, generally speaking, he's a better man than cousin rainbow, which is claiming an awful lot.

There was not a trace of crimson along the sides of the fish. He was out of water enough to show us that. There was no halting this fellow with a five-ounce outfit. When he finished his acrobatics in the air, he plunged into the center of the stream and started off for Lake Superior, with Al stumbling along as best he could and me following with my ridiculous little net. Then back upstream he came and flashed by us, a streak of living green and dim white in the murky water. We went back with him.

[31]

"My arm's getting tired, and the rod has creaked a little down near the butt," said Al. "I don't care about the rod, but I'm afraid of the leader. Get your net and try to nail him the next time he goes by!"

There's an assignment for you — try to net a big steelhead, fighting mad, with a little wire-rimmed brook-trout net! And another man's fish — perhaps the best fish he will catch that year! I began to wish I had remained asleep.

The fish fell back toward us slowly and rested for a few seconds. Al risked all and horsed him toward me. I knew it was foolish, but I tried it — slipped the net over his torpedo nose and gave a heave shoreward.

All I remember about that was the wire rim of the net bending in my hand as the steelhead, with a single smash that frightened me out of my wits, shot forward and was gone — no, not completely, for when I looked again the rod was whipping madly once more and Al's arm-weariness was showing more plainly than ever in his face. But there was still hope. His lower lip was practically merged with the tip of his nose — I mean Al's lower lip!

"Get my net!" directed Al.

I unharnessed it from his shoulder while he held the steelhead. All the time he was grunting. He grunts like that when he shoots ducks — the only grunting sportsman in captivity.

I stood there with the net like a ninny. More folly, I thought; but Al knew the strength of that leader. I knew that if we lost him I'd catch it, but "orders is orders" in a case like that.

Once more the steelhead was coaxed toward us, and once more I corraled him in the net, with his big tail and half of his body waving in my face. For the second time the net rim bent, but this time we were not so fortunate. The big fellow darted directly between my legs, and in my haste to get out of the way I fell flat on my face in three feet of water. As I scrambled ashore I felt the line entangled about my wader leg, and I had presence of mind enough not to stand up straight and anchor my leg to the bottom, for that would have given the steelhead something solid to pull on.

There was only one thing to do — get ashore on all fours, like a submarine, kicking that leg violently as I went, to free the line. My fly box dropped out of my wader pocket, and I made a dive for it just as I realized the line was free. I caught it and finished the job of swimming ashore.

It was only a miracle that permitted me to disentangle the line, and Al had the fish fighting the rod again when I brushed the water from my eyes and looked. He was laughing like a maniac, partly at the spectacle I had presented and partly at the relief of knowing that the steelhead was still on.

"What'll I do now?" Al called to me.

"Call out the marines, if you want to," I replied. "I'm not going to let any steelhead drown me."

"He'll just have to tire himself out, and it's all up to the leader," said Al.

Time after time Al worked the steelhead to within five or six feet of him, and the fish was obviously tiring, but closer than that he would not come. The pressure was kept up until he began rolling. He looked like a peeled popple log there in the waning daylight. Then, very carefully and with increasing speed, he was coaxed toward a sandbank. I walked around in back of him to take another dive after him if worst came to worst, but he was worn out after his 20-minute fight. Al grabbed him quickly by the gills and snaked him ashore. Then we both fell on him!

"What kind of a spinner fetched him out of his hole?" I asked.

For answer Al reached into the steelhead's mouth and pulled out — a long-tailed No. 8 bucktail fly.

"I knew this old mule was down here," he said. "There's always one good one in this pool. He bosses the hole, and if you throw enough stuff at him he's going to get mad finally and come out for a fight."

"Well, we were both right," I said. "But I suppose you would rather have fished here all day."

"Makes no difference to me," the old maestro answered. "I'll get 'em if I get mad enough — upstream or downstream."

And that's no fable.

*The next story is unique because it gives a
fascinating glimpse into the past. Live decoys
or "tollers" as they were called were banned in
1936 when the drought of the Depression years
struck down waterfowl numbers. Before then
every serious waterfowler had a pen that contained
ducks, mallards usually, and Canada geese in areas
where those birds were hunted.*

*The birds were tethered with leather thongs
around one leg. And they were set out in the
decoys on iron rods with a six-inch-round platform
just under the surface for them to rest on. Like
Min and Bill they were highly individualistic. Not
all would call and birds that were vocal were highly
prized. They made for lazy hunters too, as the
story indicates. With their tremendous eyesight
and perhaps hearing, the tollers would see birds in
the air long before the hunters would. The calls
alerted you to incoming birds.*

*The title, of course, comes from a highly popular
song of the era.*

Minnie The Moocher

This is the story of Min, the mallard hen with the wanton wabble, and Bill, her mate, who stayed at home while Min walked the streets.

Praises have risen upward for many moons in adulation of inspired setters that held their point in drenching rain. Lyric poems have been dedicated to gallant Chesapeakes that breasted the icy tide to retrieve distant ducks. Never have I read a deserving tribute from a duck hunter who modestly thrust the crown aside and said: "Give the credit to Susie. She brought 'em in."

Min and Bill, to whom I owe a shooter's debt of gratitude, brag an ancestry first recorded by man five years ago, when a pair of wild mallards, winging over a rice bed near Frederic, Wisconsin, was slightly wounded. One day an errant newspaper man came that way, and Min and Bill, of the fifth generation, departed the humdrum farmyard for a nobler, broader destiny. Fat they were then and complacent with the open-handed largess of the farmer, but their beady eyes and stiff-poised necks, as they hovered on the edge of the hoggish domestic fowl, gave promise that all of the wildness had not been bred out of them.

With the unexplainable caution that makes the mallard what he is in wisdom, they resented the farmer's aproach and headed for the river. Two long, perspiring hours were spent in corraling them in a cornfield. They were clapped into a box. Before the hunt was over the farmer had suggested shooting them, thinking I wanted them to eat. That was vetoed. I

[35]

wanted them for something grander than that.

Upon being incarcerated, Bill immediately showed the stuff he was made of. While Min crouched in the bottom of the crate, as befits the lesser half of well-regulated households, Bill stiffened his snake-like neck and produced blood-curdling growls and ghastly hisses.

Now, here was something. While I haven't handled many live decoys, I never yet heard of a drake that growled. I've heard of 'em hissing and mee-amphing, but not growling. Bill growled — make no mistake about that. He growled about the way an angry dog the size of a springer spaniel might growl if his bone were about to be taken from him. If you placed your finger threateningly over the crate, he would raise a belligerent eye upward, fix his stare on the finger and growl until the finger was withdrawn. Accompanying this little ceremony was a lifting of the feathers along the back of his neck.

I was afraid to tell people about it. They wouldn't believe me. I consulted local duck authorities about the matter. They said they never knew a duck to growl, and mighty few of them knew of one that hissed. That, they asserted, was common among geese, but not ducks. So I went to the President of the Old Duck Hunters' Association, Inc. If he didn't know, he might have some kind of an explanation anyway. And it was important that I tell him about the growl, because Min and Bill were going to live in his back-yard, now that Mrs. President was all through with her cold frame. Out of consideration for the President, I didn't want him to take sudden fright when walking through his own yard at night.

"So you've got a duck that growls?" he asked, raising his eyebrows.

"I have, your honor."

"H-m-m-m," he h-m-med. "Well, I was afraid of something like that. You lie about the fish you catch, and I suppose it's only natural for that same undermining tendency to carry over into the duck season."

He strode out to the cold frame, muttering something about the "amazing untruthfulness of the younger generation."

However, I proved it to him, and Min and Bill won a place in his heart instantly. We had intended to get another hen to assist Min with her main services, but the President would have none of it after hearing Bill growl.

"What?" he demanded. "You want to introduce a triangle into a family like that? I'll guarantee that when that downtrodden hen gets out there in front of the blind alone she'll tell everything she knows about Bill — and that ought to be quite a bit. Look at her there now, slinking over in the corner, and the old man in front of her, big as life, letting on how tough he is."

The President was right. Min proved to be such a gadding, gabbling creature that it was apparent we didn't need another talker. And we carefully avoided a triangle, but at that time hardly realized what lay in store for us later on, when a browbeaten Min became the central figure in a scandal that is still being quacked about in the rice beds of Washburn County.

Min had about her constantly the frightened, timid air of an overworked household slave. Bill, just as wild or wilder, did not, however, lose his swaggering front. While Min would cower and cringe before an upraised hand, Bill would growl and strike at it with his bill. It was very obvious who wore the trousers in that family.

Their first separation, on the opening day of the season, when Bill was hidden in the blind and Min was tethered out front, was heartrending. Min wanted to get back to that crate. No sooner did she realize that the comforting growl was now located in a clump of brush to which she could not swim than she called upon whatever gods watch over ducks to witness the shamefulness, the helplessness, the loneliness of her plight. She paddled to the end of her tether, took a nervous drink and raised her voice in such a quacking symphony that Joe Hollis, a mile away, heard it and sneaked in behind the big island to see what the devil was going on in the rice.

The President of the O.D.H.A., Inc., suggested tentatively during her first sufferings that maybe we ought to tie Bill out there with her for a while to ease their parting and then bring him in again. If ever there was a picture of wifely bereavement, it was presented by Min; but shortly the plot thickened.

It didn't take Min more than fifteen minutes to learn the folly of her widow's weeds, and the President and I witnessed then what might be termed by cynical people a typical act of fickle femininity. She ceased bawling and croaking for the lost mate. She ceased reaching for the rubber bracelet that held her, and she ruffled her feathers and cast her eye about for immediate assuagement of her grief. I rather think the play girl in Min came out at that moment. Maybe the bitter memory of a life of slavish subordination to Bill's whims rushed over her. The President said he thought that's what happened. He said any woman would have done the same thing if she had lived with a guy like Bill.

[37]

The eternal cunning of the female in need of companionship asserted itself when a flock of wary black ducks topped the big hill and wavered her way. Min paddled to the end of her teather and lifted up her voice in coyly worded invitations that doubtless gave promise of fine opportunities for hospitality and five o'clock tea. Afterward the President declared she was telling the strangers the old man was home keeping house and she had the afternoon off.

The blacks, interested but cautious, circled the set-up once. To prove her friendliness, Min gabbled cosily, up-ended and fed demonstratively. It was too much for the strangers. They came zooming in, and three learned a lesson in over-eagerness that was of no further use to them.

To one of the slain blacks the President, holding him admiringly at arm's length, spoke: "And you are not the first man to meet disaster because of a lady's tongue."

Hardly were we settled in the blind when a flock of green-winged teal, closely bunched, came squirting by. Min, taken aback at their sudden appearance out of nowhere, swung into action and called them back. She brought them to the very gates of hell, for they landed in the decoys. As we stood up they leaped into the air in two little bunches. Five remained behind, thanks to Min's help.

Min was beginning to like her work. She called to anything that flew. She called kingfishers, the hussy. She called crows; she called two big blue herons that croaked about an impending doomsday as they came by. She called two flocks of yellow-legs, and she called a murderous marsh hawk, which for a moment made her wish she was off the street and back in the crate with Bill — growl and all. But the hawk was killed, and the yellow-legs stuck around and played in the shallows, and Min went ahead, like the Lorelei, luring good men to their death.

Min's metamorphosis from a subdued, cringing housewife to a seductive houri of the rice beds gave the President and me great hopes. The season had started auspiciously. Our favorite pond, nearly a half mile long, had shrunk to a mass of reeking lake bottom during the dry summer.

Where, five years ago, we had rowed our boats in three feet of water, now bulged the ugly heads of muck bottom, with only here and there a stretch of water big enough to accommodate a flock of ducks. It was over one of these small remainders of a once-famous duck rendezvous that we were shooting this year. If Min continued to deliver the goods, the early mallard and teal shooting problem was settled.

Min certainly rose to the occasion in a big way, Single-handed, on that opening day, she let loose her wiles on the summer-fed mallards and blacks. At sundown the President and I had no complaint whatsoever to make of the bargain we had made with the farmer. And this kind of shooting had been obtained where, even with live decoys, it had not been easy to decoy mallards. Add to Min's glory the fact that our blind that day was no work of hunter's art, but a five-foot contraption that jumped out of the flat sand like a farmer's silo.

She was undoubtedly the best caller we had ever had. Her energy was amazing. Many callers are prone to quack a good deal when first set out, but lose their zest for the game and sit humped up on their stools, wishing someone would come along and take them in out of the wet. Min gave herself no rest. If a wing appeared in the distance, she went to work, and at 5:00 P.M. on that first warm day of the season she was calling as valiantly as she had been when we put her to work four hours before.

And so it went, from one shoot to the next. Always there was Min out front uttering the siren call of her kind, with dour Bill hidden in the blind growling at the whole performance. How many tense hours of peering and neck twisting Min gave us cannot be calculated. We did no great amount of watching for ducks when she was in the lobby collecting tickets. We sat and talked, and when she began to quack in that anxious penetrating voice it was time enough to peer cautiously from the blind. The simple fascination of watching her, alternately preening herself and searching out tidbits, was often sufficient to keep interest alive in what might have been a dull half hour or so.

As the season progressed Min became more used to her work, but never did she cease to struggle and bite when we picked her out of the crate. The wild would not be lived down, no matter how much corn she got or how much gentle stroking. She accepted them, but that was all. She would be terrified at our close approach, but once tethered in front of the blind her love of companionship quickly replaced whatever inferiority complex Bill had produced in her while she was with him.

The crowning episode in Min's not too respectable career came on a white-frost morning twenty minutes after we put her on the job. She had been strangely silent for about five minutes; then I heard a familiar quacking about three hundred yards away. I ran to the water's edge and found Min had broken away. A weak strand in the string that held her

had given way, and Min was out there somewhere in the rice.

Then the quacking grew stronger, coming our way. We saw through the dim morning light, Min flying into the decoys. Her gait was slightly wabbly but surprisingly strong for a bird that had not flown for months.

"She's repenting," whispered the President. "Thought she'd leave Bill and the whole humdrum life, but decency wins."

I sneaked out and got behind her. Finding herself cut off, she immediately leaped into the air and flew out of my sight. There was nothing domestic about the way she flung herself into the air. Before I knew what she was doing, she was twenty feet over my head and still climbing. Then she straightened out and departed.

"You settled it for her," said the President. "She thought she might tolerate Bill, but she won't stand for you. If that erring woman comes back, I'll buy you the best cigar in town. Now, if that were Bill, he'd stick around. He might run down to the pool hall for a little loafing, but he'd come back. Not Min. If there's a Salvation Army corps over in that rice bed, they can do a lot of good work right now for her."

We heard Min's strident call resound over the marsh for five minutes, heard the answering quacking of other hens. Then all was quiet.

"Gosh," said I, "I never dreamed she could fly that high."

"She's probably flying higher right now that she ever did before," ventured the President.

The morning passed, and Min cameth not back. We picked up the decoys, bundled Bill, growls and all, into the boat and rowed in for a noon lunch. By 3:00 P.M. we were back in the blind ready for whatever action there might be. Although there had been quite a few mallards flying in the morning, we had decoyed none of them. How we missed Min! As an added incentive for Min's return we staked Bill out forty feet from the blind, in plain view on the sand.

Over there in the rice somewhere was Min, getting acquainted. We speculated whether or not she were strong enough to follow the flocks southward. I thought not, although her ability to fly had amazed me when I had tried to catch her on the beach that morning.

The afternoon stretched into near sundown. The red ball of the sun was falling fast in the west behind the distant pines and maples. But no Min. We got not a shot during the afternoon. Bill's growlings and mee-amphings had no effect whatsoever on the high-flying local ducks. It was hospitality of the fireside brand which Min offered that they were looking for.

In one flock, flying low some distance away, I thought I detected Min, straggling along at the end of the procession, but could not make sure of it. The President was positive it wasn't Min. If it had been she, he contended, she would have brought every one of those ducks right in to us.

We were about to pick up the outfit and set out for home when the President crouched lower and cried: "Mark! Single on the left!"

I could not make out the incomer at first and saw the President adjusting himself for a quick rise and a shot over the blind. Just as he stood up, I got a good look at the duck, flying strongly but with legs dangling.

Those legs looked tired. And there was a familiar air about the duck. I shouted to Mr. President to wait, and he lowered his gun. And in flew Min, as big as life. The tired old lady flopped into the very spot where her tether had held her that morning.

We watched. Bill growled.

"What a tongue-lashing she's going to get!" whispered Mr. President.

"She seems glad to be back."

"Bill's a fool if he takes her back," offered the President.

"But she's here, and she wants to stay."

Min cautiously waddled ashore. Her spirits drooped. And she didn't seem to be so sure about walking up to where Bill was tethered. I got up and staked Bill farther away from the blind. She swam about in the decoys while I completed the job. Then she slowly approached Bill once more. He was far enough away from the blind so that our presence in it could not have frightened her much. But still she was doubtful.

"Quack, quack," she said by way of peace offering.

"Mee-amph. Mee-amph," answered Bill.

For some minutes they kept up a desultory conversation.

"She's telling him where she's been and what she's been doing," I whispered to the President.

"Like hell she is," he retorted. "She's telling him what a swell guy he is. What she's been doing isn't repeated, even in duck circles."

"She sure wants to come back home and be forgiven."

"Bill's a sap," pronounced the President. "For all his growlng, he's just another weak-kneed husband. Now, twenty years ago a wife caught in such a predicament was thankful if all she got was a black eye. The rising generation has changed all that. He'll take her back to his bed and board again and like it. And unless we get a new tether string for Min, she'll be

[42]

looking forward all week long to these week-ends. Once a woman starts that way, there's no stopping her."

The President and I watched the reconciliation for about fifteen minutes. By degrees Min found her way to the side of her surly spouse. Everything was all right with Bill, it seemed. He was glad to see her. His vibrant mee-amphs were contentment in themselves. Min remained very close by his side. This seemed to flatter him. After a while Mr. President and I swooped down on her. She surrendered with surprising quickness. A few feints at the water, then a quick retreat to the jackpine cover where she could not move rapidly, and she was back in her old role as Bill's wife, safe in the box with him.

From that time on, we saw to it that Min was securely tethered. Her overtures were none the less vociferous and productive of ducks. Doubtless she carried the memory of her one fling, but she's had her day. After that she behaved herself. And despite her one flagrant divergence from the straight and narrow, Mr. President and I shall always think of her as a friend who took pride in her work and brought in the ducks.

"Queer how the wildness stays in 'em after five generations in a farmyard," I remarked to the President on the way home the day of Min's adventure. "It's hard to believe she could recognize her own kind in those strange mallards."

"Strangers?" exclaimed the President. "They may have been once, but not any longer! Not any longer!"

The year was 1936. MacQuarrie has left the Superior, Wisconsin newspaper where he started his career and moved to the Milwaukee Journal. As its outdoor editor for 20 years, he was known throughout the state and, of course, from his popular stories (they were almost always featured on the covers of the magazines they were in) he had a nationwide reputation.

He's back on the Brule again here. It never ceases to amaze me the way he can so instantly transport the reader to the places he loved and the things he loved doing. For many authors, the actual writing is a chore. But I can't believe MacQuarrie's doesn't thoroughly enjoy sliding those flies down the pools or bringing those browns and rainbows up to smack at his fly.

In Quest Of The Lukewarm Beer

"You are an unregenerate back-slider," said I to the President of the Old Duck Hunters' Association, Inc.

"You bet your life I am," he answered spiritedly.

"You are," I went on, "a hypocritical rascal without principle or virtue of any kind in your mangy hide."

"Right again," agreed the President.

"One week ago, with a 4-ounce rod and 12-foot leaders, you caught as nice a mess of trout as any man could wish for on a dry fly. Is that correct?"

"Positively."

"And now you hide from my sight on the other side of my car, here on the banks of the Brule River, and hitch up a cast of wet flies on a 6-foot leader for to fish the same."

"Dog-goned if you ain't right, sonny."

"'And you have nothing to say for yourself?"

"Nothing. Only that I am weak. And I love a wet fly. I love to dunk a wet fly and get 'er down in thar where the fishes is."

"And what is that you have on the dropper?"

"That, my boy, is a dog-eared Yellow Sally, about size No. 6, if my eyes ain't gone back on me."

"And the other one?"

"Why, ain't you ever seen a Royal Coachman, No. 8, before?"

"And you're actually going to fish in this low, clear water with that

outfit?"

"Yep! I'm goin' right down that path, through them alders, down the steep bank, and I'll hit the crick just about twenty yards below the old bridge. Then I'll wade in about to my stomach and lean back agin' the water and light my pipe while the riggin' soaks up good. After that it's dunk, dunk and dunk again, straight downstream, takin' 'er easy, and by and by something's goin' to take-a-holt."

"I hope that fast water bowls you over. Any fisherman, after scaling the dry-fly heights, who resorts to such childish devices ought to drown."

"Don't get flustered, sonny," retorted the President of that revered and august body of anglers and hunters. "While I'm down there doin' things you'll be downstream a ways, diggin' in your pocket for that leetle bottle of oil and them there leetle scissors — say, they are cute. And you'll be buckin' the current and fightin' all the fast water and wonderin' where that No. 14 bivisible went after you slung 'er out."

"But it isn't all fast water. Some of it is perfect in the still places for a floater, and that's where I'm going."

"Be that as it may," retorted the Association potentate, "I'm goin' to fish wet and big and colorful and traditional. I may be a backslider, but I love the art and science of floatin' 'em downstream and draggin' 'em back — with little jerks, you know."

"Idle banter — mere idle banter," I replied. "And I'll stake my reputation on it."

"Your reputation?" The woods rang with his laughter. "Shucks, man, you ain't got no reputation. You're a fisherman."

"All right, I ain't. But I've got a bottle of beer in the back seat of the car."

"Now you're talkin' my language!"

"It's a bet, then, and the pay-off is on trout?"

"I'm off in a burst of derisive laughter," cried Mr. President, and the last I saw of him he was clomping into the brush in his waders in high glee.

It took me longer to get ready, and I had time for thought. The President is not a finished fly caster, either wet or dry. But he's a fish-getter. That previously-mentioned night on the Upper Brule, he had done great damage with my light rod and long leaders, although I could remember no cast that was laid out right. He is a sloppy caster — that's it. But dog-gone it, he gets fish, and maybe he had something up his sleeve this time.

I proceeded down an old right-of-way of lumbering days for a scant half mile, made my way through the brush and down the steep bank and hit the Brule just above the old stone dam near the ranger's cabin in Brule State Park, not far from the town of Brule. Ask about it, you fishermen, when you make your pilgrimage to that river. Of course, you will fish this famous stream sooner or later. Everyone does.

I had before me two hundred yards of beautiful dry-fly water before striking the tail of a 150-foot rapids. If I were to get that bottle of beer, I felt it would have to be done in that placid stretch, with just a hint of swirling current here and there. The stream runs north and south at this point.

The east bank is no good. In places there the water is shallow and silty on the bottom. At the west bank, calling for a right-curve cast, there is deeper water, shade and old logs, and you can stand in the middle and work it without wading too deep. The place the President fished was above me some distance, all fast water, as beautiful a stretch of wild, rugged river as you will see anywhere in the Middle West.

It seemed too easy. Good dry-fly water. Twelve-foot leaders with plenty of gut in the first six feet to make 'em lie out, an 8-foot 4-ounce rod delicate as a butterfly's breath but with the kick of a mule as you lift the D line off the water. Yes, it would be easy, I mused as I shook up a No. 14 Badger Bivisible in the "leetle bottle of oil."

Let's see now. The sun is still high and in my face, and I've got to be careful. But I can get inshore to the right a little and make the shade of the alders. The trout will not see me so plainly there. It'll be harder casting, though. Too much line over possible fish, but a little finesse and luck will take care of that. The bivisible goes on its first looping ride and settles just above and outside a projecting log. Good. I know that log. It's deep underneath, where the river has ducked its head to pass under. The first cast might not do it. Maybe it will take fifteen or twenty — but no mistakes now, mind you.

No. No mistakes. And there were no mistakes. Nor were there any fish. Strange. Always has been good for one. Not even a rise. Peculiar. Suppose this hot spell has put 'em down? Can't be possible. It's only early July, and the water is low but under 60 degrees. They can't all be 'way down deep. Oh well, try that run above, toward mid-stream. It would be a pool if the water weren't so fast at that point. Big rocks in the bottom. Always a little riffle on top of it. Small fly, fished carefully along its edge, ought to bring something.

Thirty casts — nothing. Forty casts — nothing. Change the fly. Try a No. 16 Black Bivisible. It's a pretty bright day. They may see it better against the blue sky. Many, many more casts. Nothing. Not even a fingerling. Not even a bouncing, bumptious dandiprat four inches long where, a few weeks before, there were hundreds and hundreds of little rainbows, keeping out of the way of bigger rainbows and browns.

Well, that is funny. Gosh, did the President know there was something wrong with my favorite stretch of the river for dry flies that day? What hidden, unwritten lore of the river had he drawn upon to decide against dry flies on such a day? Can it be possible I am ever going to learn to call my shots on this or any stream? Haven't I learned anything from twenty-four years of fishing this river? What's wrong with my fishing? Been reading too many books and not studying the river enough? No, that can't be it entirely. My dope works sometimes — specially the last few years, since I found out that floating flies are fish-getting flies.

I worked the whole of the stretch, but in its entire length saw neither fish nor fin. There was no visible hatch upon the water. Where had they gone? Oh well, try it over. So I plodded back down to the upper side of the dam and went through the same motions. I went through my fly book from top to bottom. I anointed them all with care. I cast them all with the greatest caution. Never, I felt, had I worked so hard to make a fly lie right. And they were lying right. But the fish were not there.

So I sat on the big rock at the foot of the 150-foot rapids and let the sun beat on my neck. It was quite hot, and I was tired. I was also licked. Might hang around until just before dark, but that was too late, and who wants to stumble around in the dark getting back up that hill? No use to go back over that stretch. Could fish it wet, but that's no fun. And that's the only reason I don't like wet flies. Maybe they'll catch more fish sometimes. I just happen to be one of those fool fishermen who like to see a fly float, and so I float 'em.

What to do? What would, say, Mr. LaBranch do? He wrote a book once about the dry fly and fast water. Did he really mean —? In that kind of water before me? In that sliding, roaring rock-chute up which I must climb to get back to the car the shortest way? He couldn't have meant that. No place to put a fly in that fast water. But is there? By golly, maybe there is.

Now, that choppy little glide just above the water-covered rocks, before she breaks into a froth? Is that kind of water fit for a floating fly? How about dropping it on there and whisking it off before it is dashed into the mixing bowl below? Easy to reach, far as that's concerned. Shucks, a tapered line will be a nuisance in there. Might as well try — it will be an experiment, though. And I never tried for a fish in that tumbling trough before with anything but a wet fly.

Off comes the 12-foot leader, and a 7-footer goes on in its place. It is the shortest I have. A No. 8 bivisible Royal Coachman is twisted on the end, and I shove off the rock into swift water. By standing at the edge I can hold my feet and reach the spot nicely. Seems kind of silly.

Wham! That word is overused but terrifically adequate. No hesitation in that kind of water. The trout saw something buggy and lammed it. Perhaps he hadn't the faintest notion what kind of fly it was. He couldn't have, squinting upward through the small maelstrom that obscured his view. But there he was, and on — hooked himself. Downstream he goes.

The strong and certain pressure of a good fish is thrilling after three hours of such fishing as I had just experienced. I'll get him easy, though. He's hooked good. Just hold him steady and let him run. No! No! Not into that faster water! It might be too much of a job to hold him there.

The trout decides for himself. He chooses the faster water — and liberty. Pound, maybe, but he felt like two. Can't use a 4x leader here. Take it off and tie on a heavier one. Coarse and over-sized it seems as I jab its point through the eye of another bivisible Royal Coachman. But it will be needed if anything hits again. Wonder if that one was just an accident. Or have I been passing up this kind of water in hot weather for years without knowing it held dry-fly fish? We'll see.

Twenty-five feet above, breasting the snatching current, there is a piece of even faster rapids, but over to my right, just beyond the fast water, is a spot, two feet wide and six feet long, that is comparatively still — so still that at its shore edge I can see down into two feet of water. If only the thrusting river would halt for a minute and let that agitated surface rest, I might see into it. But the river, rushing past, nudges the quieter water with its elbow, and it is moving — rising and falling a few inches. What little foam collects is soon swept away by the vacuum-like pull of the current on the slack water.

A trout should be there. But how to get a fly in there without having it snatched away? I edge a few cautious yards toward it until I am not more than fifteen feet from the spot. Wish I had a level line. The tapered end is

[50]

too light for a short cast, but it will have to do.

The fly goes out, and the leader has barely settled behind it when the current sweeps it away, leaving a rippling wake. Got to get closer and sneak the fly in from the side and below the hole. Only way I can float it there. I'm not a good enough fisherman to make a real slack-line cast so as to give the fly five or ten seconds of motionless life on the slack water. Five or six casts fail; then a lucky one lies just right, with a little slack. Now if the river will leave it alone a minute —

Smack! I saw that brown as he grabbed it. He came most of the way out to do it — strange tactics for the deliberate, cautious brownie, but it appears they aren't so careful when they're living in a house with shutters on it such as this one. He's out and downstream — and let him go. He can't smash that leader. He'll soon drown in the six-mile current. It is over quickly. Only 11 inches, but plump and fine.

The two fish I caught took the fly within twenty feet or less of me. So perhaps I can get closer to the next good-looking spot. It is a wave-topped area about fifteen feet square, half pool, half rapids, where the sliding water cruises into heavy bottom rocks and quick little waves are thrown up, to be gathered up quickly in the main flood.

The sun is now directly on the spot, and it is hard to see. Casting is done more or less blindly. I cannot see the fly, but those angry waters are doing things to it, I sense, as the fly remains some time in the area before being swept down to me. Maybe the fly is too small for such water. Better try a bigger one. The aluminum box in my kit avoids my fingers, and I bring up instead another little box. Little bass flies in there. I just wonder...

So a No. 6 cork body is squeezed through the neck of the fly-oil bottle and then flung into the caldron. At times, on the sun-flecked water, I can get a glimpse of the bright-hued bass bug. It twists this way and that. Evidently there are some strange current forces working on the line and leader, below the surface.

Then the fly disappears in the sun. I raise the rod lightly to see if I can bring it into vision. Instantly there comes down through the bamboo the solid, shaking tremor of a good fish. He might have had the fly in his mouth for ten seconds or so before I knew it. But he's hooked, and I raise the rod higher.

That brings him to life. He darts up through the troubled water and thrusts half his body out. For an instant he is a brilliant, writhing splash of color in the sun. Maybe he saw me, for I am very close to him. He

[51]

comes down toward me, then out to the right into water that goes strong and swift out of the demi-pool. Easy with him, now. He's a brown and knows what it's all about. Hold him from going over that lip below, and he's mine. The tackle is strong, and I net him before he is half spent, but it is just as well. The bass hook held him none too securely. A good 14 inches. He'll go a pound on a friendly scale.

I have learned something. The Brule seems to chuckle at me as I work up another thirty or forty feet. "Thought there weren't any fish in here, eh?" says the river. "Thought my browns wouldn't take a floater in this water? Ha! Ha!"

But I am satisfied with myself. A new river has been discovered. By accident or pure research I have wrested one more secret from the enigmatic Brule, and the bottle of beer looms close. Should have stuck it in the river, though. It'll be warm in that stifling sedan with all the windows and doors closed tight.

Here's another place. Over on the opposite bank the rushing river has failed to dislodge a two-foot-thick-log, embedded deep into the bank. Behind the friendly shelter of the log the river foam dances, six inches deep, two feet wide. I'll have to keep the fly below that foam. The slackline cast, even with the luck I always need on such a cast, will not do here. The water is too deep and fast for me to get closer than twenty-five feet. How about riding the fly down the edge of the fast water?

I take off the bass bug and tie on a No. 10 Brown Bivisible, for while the water there is swift it is quite glassy. The fly toboggans down the slide a half dozen times before it gets right in close to the stillwater. There it drags a bit, but not much, uncertain whether to join the current or float serenely into the foam on the backwash. The line will decide in a few seconds, when the current bellies it out and pulls the fly down. But a fish leaps into the breach and makes the decision before the river has time to act.

Rainbow this time. A rollicking dynamiter he is, taking the bivisible at the end of a nose dive that is thrill enough in itself to recompense for the whole trip. He makes for the shelter of the log, but ducks out of there quickly to have it out with me, then and there, in the faster part of the current. I seem to detect the added belligerence of the rainbow. But in that water the current is such a strong factor in the fight of the fish that it is hard to tell. I let him winnow down into the spot I have just fished, and there I can feel he has not such an advantage. Ten inches of rainbow, that's all. But it's all fighting fish, and Brule rainbows are heavy-bodied, often much thicker through the middle than browns.

Two more trout — one a brown, one a rainbow — find their way into the creel by the time I am at the top of the fast water. I have five good fish, and I have put back a dozen small ones. Hurrah! I'll guzzle that bottle of limpid beer if it turns my stomach inside out!

There is a place at the beginning of this fast-water stretch where the Brule gently nudges the bank to my right for a distance of twenty feet before toppling into sudden flight down the rocky stairway I have just ascended. I have never caught a fish there. I don't know why, but suspect it is because I cannot make the fly float right. I wonder how it would be to stand right in the beginning of the fast water, at the lip of the pool, and try a cross-handed cast. But to do it I must take off my fishing jacket, else everything in the pockets will be wet.

A new No. 12 Olive Quill replaces the bivisible, and I carefully adjust my feet to the slippery bottom rocks. I can just make it. The water burbles at my wader pocket, but my shoes are wedged solidly into bottom rocks and I can work the fly without danger of the current influencing it. I have been careful. Now I must be more careful, for the cross-handed cast is difficult for me.

A half dozen casts are made with a minimum of disturbance on the still pool in front of me. There is no give-away drag. But there is no response. Maybe I could work it closer to the bank. But to do that I've got to brave the terrors of the brush, and it would end everything if I had to wade into the pool to retrieve a stuck fly. Try it, anyway. Maybe that's why I've never got 'em here before — maybe I've been thinking too much about my precious tackle and have been unwilling to take a chance with a 20-cent fly. For shame!

I feel, as the fly goes forth towards the brush, that I am actually doing something in that spot which I have never before attempted. Will it solve the problem of that pool, which I know must hold good fish but which any fisherman will tell you is good only for night fishing? It will. It does!

The best brown of the day weaves from the shelter of the brush and takes the fly easily. Confident, deliberate, arrogant is he — the perfectly fooled brownie in the quiet pool. Two or three a year is all I ever get of his tribe in that kind of water, but they are worth more than many another taken from less difficult places.

He will not come out, but sulks under the alders. Is he hung up? I pull harder, and he yields. Upstream he goes in the quiet water. I must be careful in getting out of the fast water to follow him, or I shall be swept downstream. Let him run until you get out of this, I counsel myself. There! I gain his own quiet pool, and the sand is firm beneath my feet. What a relief from the uncertain rocks of the stairway rapid!

The brown is ahead of me about twenty-five feet. I have given him line. Now I snub him, and he comes around and downstream directly toward me. I draw my legs close together. How often have hooked fish darted between my waders! He rushes by me at close range and tries for the fast water, but I turn him and back up he goes. Now I've got him. He'll never get into that rapids. I work upstream, to keep away from the fast water. The brown is big, but not big enough to get away in that kind of water. He's mine in a few minutes.

The first fish I ever caught in the pool. Only good for night fishing, eh? And there he is, a good pound and a half. Gosh, I'm tired, after that bout with the rapids. Weary legs move toward shore, and I am about to sit on a rock when I suddenly become conscious that I am not alone. I look up. Watching me from the brush is the President of the Old Duck Hunters. He wears a Cheshire-cat grin as he comes through the alders toward me. There is, too, a look of elfish guilt upon his face.

"I've got six, and one will go a pound and a half," I declare without ceremony. "What have you got?"

"Well sir, so help me, I fished this river up and down and crosswise and never got a strike. No, sir; not a thing."

"For once, then, you have been licked." I showed him the trout.

He admitted defeat. It was a great moment for the rank-and-file membership of the Old Duck Hunters. Very seldom is it that the commoners in the organization get the best of the President. But I had done it that day. I had beat him at his own game — at the game he himself had taught me to play.

Such sweet victory comes but seldom in the life of a fisherman. Always there is some old-timer with the patience, the skill and the willingness to show him up. Always that one final barrier to perfection. But today was different. Today I was the victor.

"And now," said I, in the full flush of victory, "I shall climb that hill, pass through the brush at its top and drink the beer we left in the car."

Then did the awful supremacy of the President's position assert itself. As one who, by divine right, arrogates unto himself the fruits of the land

and the fish of the rivers, he drew himself up and pronounced: "My boy, I cooled that bottle in the river and drank it two hours ago!"

It's beginning.

"I wanted to behold the suddenly tightening grip of winter upon my beloved lakes and marshes — watch the country say its last goodby to warm wind and drowsy rain before the warm blanket of another season gently covered every dry stalk and patient pine . . . it is not all of duck hunting to hunt ducks."

Here stated in so many words is one of the emerging MacQuarrie themes, the broad focus on the outdoors, the way it looks and smells and rewards to anyone willing to accept these things.

We tend to take that view for granted these days. But remember this was written in 1936 and at a time when putting meat on a table was all important to too many people. So to leave a blind, to savor and enjoy, was a new and pioneering notion. MacQuarrie was pointing out a new and different path for sportsmen to follow.

Gallopin' Goldeneyes

The President of the Old Duck Hunters' Association, Inc., pounded mittened hands to warm them, and then widened a place in the scrub-oak blind the better to see from it. It was that solemn, hushed hour when daylight grapples with dawn on a mat of overcast skies and the final result is a draw — neither daylight nor darkness.

The last day of the season it was, and Mister President, knowing there had been severe freezing weather, had debated long before deciding to go. A ten o'clock decision the night before had sent him hurrying to the basement after his gear, and he had risen with me at 4 A.M. to flee sixty-five miles southward through the November night.

We had toted the sinews of war a solid mile around a frozen lake edge, to a thumb of land bordered with shallow water but exposed to every wind. In those winds had lain our hope that the water about the point would be open. And it was, except for twenty-five feet or so of thin ice I had easily broken through in making the set.

It was cold. Not the bluffing nips of October, but the still, steely cold of November, chilling the land for the snows to come. Ears tingled, and October gloves had given way to November mittens. The President pulled down his earlaps and pounded his hands. He said he could see ice making where I had broken a trail placing decoys and that he was darned glad the season closed when it did because he was running out of clothing to don with the falling temperature.

Neither of us was optimistic. But we'd had our mallards early in the season and harried the deep divers two weeks later when they came blasting through. Now, with potholes and many lakes frozen, we knew distinctly we were on the ragged edge. It was largely a sentimental sojourn, merely to carry on the traditions of the O.D.H.A.

It wouldn't have been right to thrust aside shotguns just because there might not be many ducks — or any ducks. The Association has no patience with such hunters. The desire had been strong to untie once more the stout cord about the neck of a lumpy decoy sack and spread wooden ducks over the face of the water.

I wanted to see, before Thanksgiving rolled around, the craning neck of Mister President once more thrusting up from the old brown mackinaw collar. I wanted to see the cleaving flight of feathered migrators splitting the wind before me. I wanted to behold the suddenly tightening grip of winter upon my beloved lakes and marshes — watch the country say its last good-bye to warm wind and drowsy rain before the white blanket of another season gently covered every dry stalk and patient pine.

The day was one for moods. The sun was somewhere behind the black, woolly mass overhead. It struck me as I watched the stingy daylight grow that it is not all of duck hunting to hunt ducks.

Impressions of many mornings in many blinds burn deep into the memory of your wildfowler. His is an exacting huntsman's trade, but no sport calling for communion with the dawn can escape a certain air of romantic mystery.

The President aroused me from my preview of a young new day to ask why we didn't have cork decoys instead of wooden ones. He was sitting on two or three of the heavier ones in a sack, and since they made awkward stools he loudly proclaimed his discontent. The President sets up housekeeping when he enters a blind. Every twig must be just so. Every old shell is picked up and piled neatly under cover. Every comfort available is put to use. This morning he had his old kerosene lantern lit and placed between his legs, over which he had spread a disreputable army blanket. Thus does he combat the rigors of the noblest sport.

Some day when he gets old I shall get a chair for him and lug it around to blinds, in order never to be without his priceless services as guide, interlocutor and interpreter of men and ducks — but he'll never grow old.

For a full half hour no broad-billed son of the north came our way. Full daylight was now upon us — a fuzzy, indeterminate grayness hanging so close to the earth that it seemed possible to reach up and poke a hole in it. The President fumbled through mackinaw, leather jacket and sweater vest for his watch. Reading the time, he grumbled that he might just as well have slept another half hour "like I told you."

The deep, gray-green lake before us, quiet as a mill-pond, bore no sign of ducks. A flock of Lapland bunting flirted about the blind for a few moments, and a friendly whiskey jay actually perched on it. The President went about his housekeeping, patting a twig here, bending one back there to make it do more work. Then he got tired of it all and opined he was going back in the woods and light himself a fire and thaw out.

He wasn't a hundred yards away from the blind when a flock of about twenty or so materialized straight out front. They didn't come from any particular place — unless it was from the clouds overhead.

My earlaps were down; so I hadn't heard them. I have come to rely on my ears almost as much as my eyes in hunting ducks. This flock was fairly low but too high to decoy on the first charge. Should I let them pass and take a chance on their circling? Ah, fateful question which every hunter must answer in his own way. Guess 'em right and you're a hero. Guess 'em wrong and you're something else.

But Mister President was in plain view, and they were in range as they swished overhead, close-packed. Maybe they would have circled. One never knows. I stood and fired.

They were directly overhead then, perhaps thirty-five yards high. In a way their sudden appearance was a triumph for patience and a vindication of my secret belief that "there still must be a few left in the country." I didn't aim at those ducks at all. I know my cheek was not on the stock. I just pulled twice and two collapsed in that spectacular plunge of the stricken duck. They hit the frozen sand beach behind the blind and when I picked them up Mister President was loping back into the blind, all thought of a fire gone from his mind.

Both were mergansers...

Might have known it. Only on mergansers do I collect with such precise finality. The President, in the blind by this time, called cheerily:

"What are they?"

"Bluebills!" I lied, and back in the blind hid them from his sight. Just to bear me out, six of these noble fowl flared before the blind and tore on down the lake. For bluebills the Honorable President will keep me company. For mergansers he will go and light a fire.

I wish you might have seen him on a dead run for that blind. Dignity of office was cast to the winds. On his face were written sheepishness and guilt and jollity all in one, which is a way the President has of disavowing a blunder.

If I make a mistake, like showing myself too much at a strategic time, the President bawls me out. If he misses an easy one, he says it was my fault anyway. And that is the way it should be in any well-governed organization.

He was all for hunting now. He'd seen ducks. When an empty sky suddenly produces winged game the President is wont to stick out his under-jaw and yell "Lemme at 'em!" I've kept him on trout streams once or twice by reporting fictitious strikes, although such tactics are not often necessary. Usually the difficulty is in getting him to start for home.

He either wants to quit right now, dammit, or stay until after the last dog is hung. I've learned to exercise a very delicate control over him when he gets in one of his quitting moods. Thus has been effected a normal condition — moderation and perserverance are properly conjoined.

All business now. In the manner of a quick fellow with weapons, Mister President showed me how quick he was on the draw — pulling his hand out of a mitt. He said it took years of practice to do it right, and then bet me a cigar he could beat me, which he did. I discovered only after he got my cigar that he had snudged by removing the woolen liner in his own mitt. And he was the referee, too.

But finally he said he hadn't come out to put on a vaudeville show and was going to "look some ducks." He does this by wiping his horn-rims very carefully with a blue handkerchief and then just looking hard through them, I've seen him "look" ducks out of nothing on bluebird days. He turns his head constantly from side to side, squinting and muttering all the while. If this fails he has a sure-fire method. He just stands outside the blind in plain view and pretends that he isn't duck hunting. It's bound to bring ducks.

In about fifteen minutes of hard work he "looked" a flock of ten. As he sank to his knees he admitted he'd bored a hole through his glasses, but — "there's your ducks." There they were, all right, lowering into our lake. They vanished for a moment into the black-green background of the pine woods shores. Then I caught them again, limned against the brighter water, not twenty feet above it. They had apparently seen our decoys long before we had seen them and were coming spraddling in, wings set for the long glide, then flailing powerfully as they flung themselves back for the landing.

Their charge into the decoys had been so sudden and direct that we did not take the easy incoming shot. We had thought they might circle at least once. So Mister President stood up and said, "Hey, youse guys!"

As they skittered up I saw they were golden-eyes. Big, cleanly-marked birds. Is there any duck whose breast against the sky is so white and broad as that of the golden-eye?

We downed two as they tore for safety, and I hurried through the shallow water to pick them up before they drifted into deep water. In the light rising wind one floated out of reach of boots. It would be picked up across the lake. We had no boat. Knowing that place, we had decided a boat would be only an unnecessary encumbrance on a trailer at the early hour of our departure from home. To such fineness of detail has the technique of the O.D.H.A. been worked out.

The retrieved golden-eye was a drake. As I inspected that first drake I felt that somewhere in the northern fastness where he dwells there must be a duck valet who lacquers his short bill, shines his yellow shoes, grooms the snowy, immaculate breast and, as a final touch, affixes the round white boutonniere just below either eye.

For trimness with speed, for power with grace, no duck — not even the wedge-faced canvasback — has anything to beat the golden-eye.

Back under cover and well started arguing with Mister President that "I did too kill one of those ducks," we were halted when a growing whisper came to my ears, now freed of their muffs. I heard 'em a half-mile away.

And why not? Not for nothing does the golden-eye put his muscular body against those scimitar wings. No duck that flies carries a sweeter song. All ducks are whistlers to some degree, but the golden-eye's powerful pinions place him in the front row of the celestial choir.

Through the President's own private porthole in the blind I saw them — a line of pulsating dots and dashes as they lowered into our lake. There may have been a hundred in the squadron.

"Holy smoke!" breathed the President. "That's more golden-eyes than I ever saw in this country in one flock — if they're golden-eyes."

They were golden-eyes. The whistling of wings grew to a hollow, tearing roar as some of them stiffened for the quick slide in. But there were other and wiser ones among them, and these bore off so that all circled away. Their piercing whistle diminished, then rose suddenly louder and shriller as they wheeled abruptly and came smashing back into the blocks. Then the searing "ha-a-a-a-sh" of outspread wings. This time there was no hesitation.

They were coming in!

They're in!

The story has often been told and lost nothing in its repetition. Or maybe it's a new story every time it happens. Maybe every new dauntless breast before a 12-gauge is distilled drama as sweet as honey, as right as rain.

When the unpromising sky grows suddenly electric with singing wings, all of the little anticipations and hopes of the duck hunter are gathered into a brilliant flash of supreme sport. And though no duck falls the hunter has had his moment and the day is a good day.

I didn't unlimber right off. There were things I had come to see besides ducks. I was fascinated by the intensity of Mister President. He arose in one cat-like move and his feet were firm when he stood. His chin was out at that familiar angle. As he stood, the black leather mitt on his right hand fluttered significantly downward. Then his lean cheek went down on varnish and the automatic spoke three times, with deadly cadence.

And three blurred plummets from the zooming flock edged into my vision as I tried to follow the others, moving to our left. My first barrel found one and the second plucked out another from the rear. When I returned from the pickup — two floated beyond reach — Mister President was reloading with the thrifty air of a man who likes to make a shell do its chore without fuss or bother.

The President and I have hunted ducks from September to mid-December in these Upper Wisconsin counties through many years. We think we have seen them all fly by. Once on a Burnett County lake we had sixteen ducks in a day's shooting and twelve different varieties. But golden-eyes in such numbers were a new experience for both of us.

This is not a golden-eye country. Some tarry about Lake Superior and along some rivers all winter but they are, up this way, a straggler species. Often they'll be shot as singles, and strangely enough they are devilishly hard to decoy as singles — especially wise old drakes.

We connected their appearance with the greater than usual number of mergansers everyone killed here this season. The Upper State had a peach of a merganser pogrom from the opening to the end. I know many hunters who gave up in disgust at repeatedly knocking down mergansers, but the

President and I were always glad to contribute our doses of chilled sixes to those dragon-heads as partial payment for a fish they had guzzled. We wondered if the curtailment of seasons recently has had anything to do with the merganser increase.

Neither the President nor myself has any delusions about the flavor of golden-eyes. The solemn truth is they are not as good in the roaster as most other deep divers. Unquestionably their fishy diet tends to make their flavor strong. But if they are hung a week, soaked in vinegar and water and then roasted with an onion inside, it will take an expert to decide what they are. Also, their flavor varies greatly. We have eaten some almost as mild as mallards and others very strong.

The thing to do is play safe and treat them all alike — hang 'em, soak 'em and onion 'em.

By shortly after noon we had nine ducks. "Two for you and seven for me," announced the Hon. President, making an official tally.

"And how about those two bluebills I shot?"

"They're the ones I mean," said Mister President. "Let's see 'em."

He dragged out the hidden mergansers and eyes me sorrowfully.

"And you like ducks so well, too," he sympathized.

The President was duck crazy by this time. In a few years he'll sprout pinfeathers. His wife says he sits up in bed o' nights and waves an imaginary shotgun over the foot after a day in a blind. Gone was his lassitude of early morning. He held the chair with all the dash of arrogance that befit his many years as presiding officer. If I were to garner any glory that day it would have to be somewhere else.

So I took a walk. Taking a walk while hunting from a point blind is often the best part of the day. It warms one. It gives a new viewpoint. Coming back to the blind is like returning home from a long journey — especially if Mister President is keeping house there.

I hiked around the shore, picked up the ducks which had drifted across in the light breeze, hung them where they would be found easily on the return trip, and kept right on going around the lake.

At this place there is a little creek connecting "our" lake with another. The second lake was frozen but maybe the creek would be open. This creek, not more than seventy-five yards long, flows both ways, depending on height of water and recent rains. There isn't a tree anywhere near it, but its banks and the creek itself are grown up heavily to weeds and low water growths.

Could there be a mallard or two left there in that shallow water? It hardly seemed possible, but anything's possible to a duck hunter. Sure enough, the creek was open. I patrolled the bank but no mallard or black duck started up. A month before they had fed over that shallow little lake by the hundreds.

A single crow crossed overhead. I shot and missed. Then, almost from under my feet, soared a dozen mallards, and there I was, with one shell left. I must have been within twenty feet of them a moment before. They had skulked quietly, loath to leave the little creek. It was impossible to miss with the remaining shot and one squawking hen dropped to the creek.

One mallard was better than none. Why hadn't I combed that spot more closely? A double on such a takeoff would have been a snap. Next time I'll know enough to throw rocks into such cover before passing it up. I retraced my steps, added the golden-eyes to my load and got back to Mister President.

"Yuh got a mallard, eh?" was his greeting as I came up.

"Yep."

"But yuh shot twice."

"Missed a crow."

"Humph!"

"A dozen got up."

I knew the minute I said it I should have kept still. He was on me like a hawk.

"Sure, I know. They got up out of the creek hole when you shot at the crow and you had only one shell left. And you're the guy who's been runnin' agin' me for president for the last five years!"

"Go try it yourself then! They'll likely come back. It's the only shallow water I know of hereabouts."

"In one hour," intoned the President, fumbling again for his watch, "I'll go over there to your pothole and knock me down a couple of fat mallards."

"If you do, you're President again by acclamation."

Then he declared a noon recess for lunch, baited me further over the fire we built, and allowed there wasn't a mallard in these parts he didn't know by his or her first name. The upshot of it was, he started off at about 2:30 in the afternoon, leaving me to keep tab on the golden-eyes.

"The score," he declared on his departure, "is now seven to one. Pretty soon it'll be nine to one."

Three hundreds yards from the blind he was when a pair of golden-eyes burst in on me. Both got away unscathed. Mister President stopped to watch, and when the pair dusted away he shouted:

"The score is still seven to one!"

There is no use arguing at a distance of three hundred yards. I settled down. An hour passed. An hour alone in a duck blind is a long time when no duck comes along. Then I heard two shots from over near my creek — then a single after-shot. Wounded one, anyway. Maybe he had two, the old rascal. And he'd given 'em plenty of time to return. Probably had waited for them and had bellied up to them after they came back.

About a quarter of four I picked up the decoys. Reluctantly I tied the cord about the neck of the sack. Reluctantly I piled the gear in one heap near the blind. How one hates to call it quits for a whole year!

By and by I saw him coming. It was getting very cold and the low clouds were finally delivering their threat of snow. Fine scattered volleys there were blown away in the gathering nor'wester. The President's bearing was jaunty. At the blind he pulled two fat mallards from under his old brown mackinaw.

"There is," intoned Mister President, "a motion before the house that I be again elected President of the Old Duck Hunters."

I was thinking of an answer when he went on:

"The membership has voted. All in favor of a unanimous choice say 'aye.'"

"But —," I began.

"Carried!" shouted the President.

*I would call the next story meat & potato
MacQuarrie. Mr. President gets lost trying to find
the stream and has to wrestle a grizzly crossing the
Cascades. Mac misses a big brown that waved his
fist under the angler's nose and was gone. Dry fly
fanatic MacQuarrie is caught digging worms, at
Mr. President's order, of course. After all afternoon Mr. President comes in tired and disgusted
and fishless . . . and then. I'll let MacQuarrie
tell it.*

Standard fare.

Go Marengo!

Now in Ashland, Wisconsin, dwells one of the name of Schiller, christened Roy. It was inevitable that the President of the Old Duck Hunters' Association, Inc., and I should one morning, halt our car in front of his house at the hour of 6:30. Though Roy is not a man given to exhortation, he had for some time been pointing and persuading.

"Come," he had said, "to the Marengo River, and I'll show you brown trout in numbers beyond your fondest dreams."

This declaration he repeated from time to time during the winter, despite the fact that Mr. President had tested Roy's ardor by explaining that he was afflicted with nightmares in regard to trout streams and so was inured to the crass realism of disappointment in such matters.

The night previous to our departure from Superior for Ashland, Roy and the Marengo, Mr. President approached me apologetically.

"I'm busy tonight," he had said. "Would you mind digging a few worms for me?"

He said it quickly and then got out of earshot before I could reply. For these many years I have done missionary work with this man and have even won him over to the dry fly for months at a time. Then all of a sudden he backslides — goes on a howling angleworm spree and bobs up for the next trip apologetic but, at heart, unchastened.

There was nothing left to do but dig the worms, thus making me a party to his unregenerate ways. If I waited until just before dark, I could

[67]

prospect for them in comparative privacy in the old hothouse bed without the neighbors seeing me. Also, a lilac bush screens part of this angleworm ranch: so I was fairly safe. But an urchin passing down the alley on a bicycle betrayed me by yelling: "MacQuarrie's goin' fishin' — he's digging' worms!"

One of life's awfullest moments. Me digging worms! I was a fool just to satisfy the whim of Mr. President.

So we picked up Roy at Ashland at the hour when folk were going to early mass. There was about the man Schiller the honest, pungent flavor of citronella — a lingering fragrance which, he explained, remains with him until about August 1, when the mosquitoes aren't so bad. In his hat rim, ringing him like a halo, were sundry flies of his own manufacture, and in his bearing was that air of early-morning confidence I associate with all trout fishermen at 6:30 A.M.

The signs were not auspicious. It had rained over the whole state that night — the worst rain of the year. With two inches of it had come a knifing wind from Lake Superior which had knocked over a coal-dock, deroofed half a dozen buildings and bashed in scores of windows. Rivers we had passed on the way to Ashland were red torrents, choked with the brick-colored clay of the Lake Superior country. Fish Creek, a famous trout stream four miles out of Ashland, was very high and unbelievably discolored. It was cold, with intermittent dashes of rain and a fog blanket lying just above the earth.

Despite all these things, Roy bore himself with kingly arrogance.

"She'll be high," he admitted, "but she'll be the clearest river in upper Wisconsin today. The Marengo flows through solid granite. I've been there four times this week in the evening after I closed the store. Just smell that basket!"

Confirmatory sniffs of redolent willow withes were made while Roy leaned back and uttered further praise of his favorite river. Our destination was twenty-five miles south of Ashland. Out of the town on highway No. 24, through Sanborn, left at the school, right at the church, and from there on Roy took the wheel. It was easier than yelling from the back seat: "No, don't take that road — the other one!" At that, I believe I could fumble my way back in there with the help of a few settlers. But tell someone on paper how to get there? My only answer to that is that it's the first turn to the left as you enter Wisconsin.

Like a groom with his bride Roy swept his hand toward the river as we debarked near a narrow bridge. There was the Marengo below us, fifteen or twenty feet wide, studded with granite teeth, overhung with heavy timber, whispering the old, old story of trout, dark pools, conquest — victory! It is necessary to blurt right out here that the Marengo at this point is as beautiful a trout stream as I have ever seen. This is something like heresy to all like myself who fish the famous Brule consistently, but it must be said that the upper Marengo is a stunner.

There she comes — dark, sinuous, fast, cut through a mountain-like formation of granite with here and there igneous rock formations to abrade waders and bump knees. It rises, I am told, in a lake "'way up there somewhere — the browns go up there in August to cool off." Then it hastens on downstairs, flows through Lake Marengo, thence into the Bad River, which eventually flows into the White River and Lake Superior. Above Lake Marengo, only browns for a long stretch — then specks. Below the lake, nothing but rainbows.

We got our orders from Roy, after first making a frightful mess of the interior of the parked car, as is the custom of all trout fishermen. I have striven manfully against this slovenly housekeeping in automobiles on trout streams, but Mr. President prefers the old ways. Once I got him to put everything in a big pack-sack to sort of keep it together. Then he got two pack-sacks to take care of the stuff. But the situation hasn't changed. His stuff just overflows from those sacks. Thus, weeks after a fishing trip, his wife is likely to find a stray leader or even a stray fish in between the rear cushion and the body. This is very bad. Now you take a fish that's been dead a weak or so — but I digress.

Roy was ready first. In fact, I don't think he ever takes his boots off during trout season. He just snapped his rod together and put on a coat which is a completely equipped hardware store.

This part of the Marengo is given to bridges. There are four of them in little more than a mile. All serving little-used roads, too. Roy advised Mr. President to go upstream to bridge number three in order that he might fish downstream as he preferred. He advised me to start where I was and work up, as I had said something about dry flies. As for himself, he went off at a lope downstream from bridge number one.

So I saw Marengo. And while the browns would have none of my floaters that morning, I was continually thrilled by the beauty of the place. At a deep hole Roy had told me about I put on one of his home-made flies, a No. 8 with short-clipped deer-hair body and sparce brown hackle for deep going. In five minutes I had a 12-incher in my net, and before the day was spent I came to bless that dirty white nondescript.

This was the only brown I took as long as I fished upstream. He had a throatful of black beetles and angleworms that bulged out of his mouth as I squeezed him. That should have told me to fish deep, but I am a fool dry-fly fisherman and I have the habit, like many of that ilk, of fishing against the current with a dead fly thrown up and floated down. It just wouldn't work that way — wet or dry.

I turned over trout — maybe fifteen or twenty — and was duly impressed with the number of browns in the river, but they would not take. Three hours or more passed, and the hour of noon drew nigh. Then I met Mr. President. Despite the cold and fog, he was very hot and very bothered.

"I just now began to fish," he cried in accents wild. "What did you guys do — put up a job on me?"

I regarded him with amazement.

"I've been everywhere but here since I left you," he related. "Roy told me to take that road to get to the bridge. I took it, all right. I walked on it until it was just a trail, and still no river. Then I got on another road and walked and walked and walked. [His wading brogues weigh exactly five pounds each!] Every time I crossed a hill I expected to hit the river. I passed through a town, and dogs barked at me. People came out on porches to stare, and one fellow wanted to know what that damn fool was doing with a fish pole fifty miles from a trout stream.

"After a while," he continued wearily, but warming to his subject, "I concluded I was getting close to California and was feeling all right because I know a guy out there who would have asked me in for a drink. But it struck me suddenly that he was dead and I'd better start back. On the way back I came to a couple of Indian villages — so far back in that the owls flirt with the chickens and the Indians were in native dress. And finally I got back here, and I've just this minute begun to fish!"

Unbelievable but true! The word of Mr. President is gospel. I left him with the injunction to be at the car by one and we would eat, which we did. Roy heard this amazing tale, with variations this time and one alluring chapter in which he encountered two grizzlies and a panther while crossing the Cascades. Roy had four browns like those you see in resort catalogues. Mr. President proceeded to cut a swath through the sandwiches. He had passed up breakfast to hasten the pilgrimage to the

Marengo.

"All I had this morning was a factory girl's breakfast," he explained between mouthfuls.

"What's that?" asked Roy.

"A toothpick and a walk."

And to make matters worse, he had fallen in after I had met him.

"So far," he said, "I've fished just about thirty minutes. Yes, she's a nice river, but not for lying down in."

He regarded Roy's four fish with envy, and when we locked up the car for the afternoon attempt he whispered to me, "Where's them worms?"

Roy heard him and yanked a couple of flies from his hatband. Mr. President accepted them with thanks, but plunged into the duffel in the car to resurrect the lethal can. Then he walked away, muttering to himself.

It should be said, before going farther, that Roy Schiller is the answer to the question: who ties the best flies in Wisconsin? Now Roy is not a commercial fly-tyer and makes no potatoes out of this noble pursuit. He runs his shoe store in Ashland with appropriate devotion and fishes with a rare fire. He is not in the business of tying flies for sale. Such flies as he ties are seldom to be found for sale anywhere. I have known Roy for twenty-five years, and from the time he was a mere dandiprat there have been few to equal him in any undertaking requiring manual dexterity.

Roy fishes any way conditions demand. He is, you will learn on inquiry, just about the top fisherman over Ashland way. He fishes for anything and everything and makes 'em all take artificials. He demonstrates his art at winter clinics sponsored by Sid Gordon, Wisconsin stream ecologist, who, by the way, is doing a good job rebuilding streams in these parts.

The perfection of Roy's art is sufficient to draw wonderment from the most hardened fly-tyers. Some day I should like to enter him in a national competition. He's a guy who does things. As a kid, he could ride a bike better than anybody in the neighborhood and when he wanted anything he made it, from a pair of boots to an automobile. Just one of those incredible mechanical wizards with quick, dexterous hands and a mind to go with them.

"Have it your own way, Mr. President," said Roy. "I like flies, and I know these two will take 'em today."

So Mr. President went away, and Roy went away, and I went away — this time upstream a couple of bridges so that I could fish down. Maybe

[71]

that would work in that high, foggy river. It did! Reeling in a long line after searching a hole, a pound brown smashed Roy's clipped buck-hair, and what a time I had taking him from under a log! The water was fast, and this one loved home and fireside. I netted him and realized what they wanted was a deep, wet fly — moving. Add up that one, you fishermen who have come to associate the brown with the holy-holy floater or the dead drifting nymph.

I glowed with the pleasure of discovery. Maybe they thought it was a minnow. Or a bettle. Or maybe they knew darned well it was a Schiller fly and just hit it out of revenge.

At the next riffle I dropped it into the very center of the swift water. Oop! Was it a fish or a rock I had snagged? I hauled in the fly. It was still sharp. Back it went again. Wow! It was I who said that when he nailed it again. The hook was set, the tip held high, the slack line permitted to slide through my fingers. Then the slack was gone and he was tearing it off the reel. He was getting too close to a log jam, and I called a halt.

I had forgotten the leader was 4x — that's all. Let it pass. I reeled in and substituted a husky 1x of six feet for the 10-foot wisp which I had been using out of dry-fly habit. It was just as good. It was better — it held. The iron-colored Marengo, fast and in flood, required no such finesse as 4x leaders — not even for browns.

Around a bend I came face to face with a Marengo angler who was very busy and who seemed happy. I left the stream and went around him without comment.

I seemed to be on top of fish all afternoon. Trout ten feet away hit me incredibly, but always it was the dirty white buck-hair of Roy's they smashed. At the end of the day a little tube in which I stick used flies, to be gone over later, held a dozen or more flies — not one of which had scratched a fish.

Of course, the river was in flood. The trout were right out in the fastest parts, sometimes in water so strong that it was hard to maintain balance, and what they did to me, and for me, that day will long be remembered. Perhaps I saw or felt forty fish at the Schiller fly. They were cagey about it, but they would at least take a shot at it if I kept it moving against the current. No go on the drift cast. They just let it slide by.

A fluttering movement made them frantic. Time and again they would thresh wildly out of water, striking at the fly two, three and four times — and miss it. Hard to figure it out. Some say they are playing when they do

that. I say no. I say, in my new-found wisdom, they've beem bottom-feeding, suddenly see what they think is a top-water minnow and rapidly adjust their sights. But no one can make bull's eyes on such short notice. That also accounts, to me, for the fact that they would come back for more — which is not the way I have found Brother Brown on very many afternoons.

They will do the same thing with dry flies. You cast over 'em hard and often. Say you're working over a brown and finally get him interested. Maybe it will take fifty casts. Then he'll try it. But like as not he'll miss. I feel they have to have just so much practice before they become accurate after they suddenly change their mode of feeding. Maybe it's another fool fisherman's fancy. But I've brought 'em up with the "created hatch" idea and had 'em miss it many a time. Of course, on real dry-fly days, when he's looking surfaceward for food, the accuracy of the brown is well known. It's one of the things that makes him such a splendid dry-fly smasher. But skip it if I grow pedantic. I'm running off in a theoretical manner, and there is positively nothing theoretical about the Marengo.

The back cast had to be watched. The roll cast was best in many places, although the Marengo is by no means a creek. Short casts were usually as good as long ones. I wasn't scaring 'em any with my hobnails on the rocks, and the day was very dark, the river high, of course, and fog eddied in and about the deep granite-sided valley. By 7:00 P.M. I had a pocketful of nice brown trout, and not one fish taken was a fingerling. Only one did I put back. They averaged in size over 11 inches. They were fat and dark and hard fighters.

As I neared the bridge where we had landed in the morning I marked a V of water in front of a log jam that divided the current. The Schiller Special was drifted into the V to one side of the jam, then worked back toward me. Even now I can't believe that trout was so big. But he must have been. He came out of the water a clean foot — why, I don't know. The fly wasn't up in the air anywhere. He didn't leap out. He wallowed out — he smashed out. He was one of those shouldery porkers that the kids sometimes get on sucker bait when after big pike in such streams as the Namakagon. Well, I'll put him down at three pounds, being conservative at heart.

I waited a minute. It seemed like years there in the fog; then I repeated the performance. Again he came, in a careening, smashing flop. He didn't touch the fly. At least I didn't feel it either time. What the devil was going

[74]

on? One more roll cast down in there. Twitch it back. Jerk! Jerk! Jerk! In tantalizing cadence I worked the fly slowly back toward me, and for the third time that awful monster did barrel rolls not twenty feet away from me. Never touched the hook. He was a red and brown dervish in the foggy dusk.

Panic seized me, and I began racing through my pockets for the sinews of war. Bucktails, nymphs, a shiny black beetle, a blue-tinged dragon fly, a spinner (I bow my head in shame!) — all these I tried, but answer cameth not from the V in front of the log jam.

It was cold. It was foggy. It was sprinkling rain. My waders had leaked a little that day, and I was damp. I was also worn out from stumbling over granite. But as I left him there in the V and climbed to the bank and the car there was cold sweat on my brow.

If he had taken, I'd have lost him in the logs, no doubt. But he didn't take — yes, he did. He took hold of my throat and the seat of my pants and shook my angler's soul to its foundations. There's always one like that on a stream like the Marengo. I won't forget him, waving his fist under my nose. I quit after that. It was time to quit. A half hour of light remained, but anything else would have been an anti-climax; and further, I can stand having my heart broken only once per day.

Roy arrived at the car as I did. I had eight fish. He had an even dozen, and all of them were big enough to lay on the kitchen sink with a flourish. We lit our pipes to wait for Mr. President, who presently would come and open up the car and let us in to the assorted oddments therein.

In the dying light the fog sifted eerily over the granite, pine-clad bluffs of the Marengo. A whippoorwill abruptly commenced to sing, settling eagerly to his all-night chore. Softly comes the night along the Marengo — even on foggy days.

Then out of the fog and dusk came Mr. President. He groaned with the weight of his gear. Defeat was written on his face. He said nothing until I asked.

"Only a few little ones," he replied with a weary sigh.

He unlocked the doors of the car and began the arduous task of filing away this and that, digging out needful apparel (including my only dry pair of socks) and grunting disapproval at mankind in general. On the other side of the car I saw him fumble awhile after stowing his gear. Then he shouted to us that we could get into the car from his side. We walked around.

[75]

My foot slipped on something big and slippery as it touched the running-board. It was a fish. It was a brown trout fish twenty inches long, and stretched alongside it were half a dozen others of varying but decent proportions. The revered Mr. President chuckled in the gathering darkness. We fell upon him with a multitude of questions.

"I cannot tell a lie," he finally confessed. "I took him with a gob of worms. He came out twice and smashed a wet fly. Then I reached for the can and put on about five worms — big ones. I dressed that hook as carefully as you'd trim the family Christmas tree. Those worms looked so good I could have eaten them. I let 'er down easy and gentle, once — twice — thrice. then I worked 'er back, just e-e-e-easy and — there he was!

"Then I reached for my net. Gone, it was! Jerked off in the brush. I held him as long as I could, snaked him toward shore and as he passed me I kicked. It took him amidships. You know I've always said those wading boots of mine are too heavy. They almost killed me this morning, but they saved my life this afternoon. They plowed through the water like a torpedo, and Mr. Trout lit on the shore. Then I lit on top of him, and we wrestled it out. Boy, was he strong — had a hammerlock on me for a minute.

"Just then a wildcat came along, and I jumped on him. Took me nearly five minutes to chase him away, and then — you know how it is — I began looking around for a bear. Just one fightin' mama bear with cubs was what I needed to let the world know how I felt. And if one had come along — "

There's no use in letting him go on like that. We broke camp and hit the trail through the fog, dropping Roy at Ashland. On the main road back to Superior we got to discussing Roy's flies which, I am bound to repeat, are perfection.

"That boy certainly can tie flies," I declared.

Mr. President peered at me in the dim light from the dash and answered, "I wrap a pretty good angleworm myself."

Proceed with caution: High Jinks Ahead.
Most times MacQuarrie made the outdoors the
point and meaning of his story. Sometimes when
he has a good twist, he merely uses it for back-
ground. This yarn is almost classic in its stead
development — a clear opening, the unfolding
problem, its solution and a final kicker. Charac-
terization, the ability to make people come alive,
was another MacQuarrie knack. Nowhere is it
more apparent than here.

The Big Pothole

Up in North Wisconsin there is a big pothole lake where you can get some grand duck shooting — providing you can find the place.

The President of the Old Duck Hunters' Association, Inc., once described the route in to a non-member as follows:

"Turn right at the first school house as you enter Wisconsin. Don't ask Joe. We pay him for not telling. Keep right ahead on the sand trail, bearing to the left and sort of up and down. Park your car by the old ram-pike that was hit by lightning in 1922 and walk in from there over the trail. It's only three miles."

So forbidding was that six-mile walk, in and out, that even the few who knew of this duck Valhalla hunted it but seldom. Your Winchester farmer of Wisconsin's barren lands might tramp that far for a buck. But any well situated resident thereabouts could get ducks with less effort. Only wildfowlers of the old school, like Mister President, make a practice of going into such remote places.

However, we had evolved a go-light system which eased the labor. In the first place we took not more than eight or ten decoys in the big gunny sack and loaded our pockets with shells. Then with guns, thermos, lunch and camera we were fairly well geared for the long hike. Hikes out with a limit apiece of mallards only seemed to lighten our burdens.

There was one objection to the limited number of decoys. A setup of eight boosters required superfine work with a duck call and right there is where Tom comes into the story. His name wasn't Tom, but it'll do.

Tom was the owner and guardian of the lower end of a fine hard sand trail that would bring a car to within a quarter mile of his place. He not only owned the original quarter section he had homesteaded years back but had gobbled up other tracts nearby, for Tom was the exception that proves the rule that you cannot farm the scrub oak barrens of Wisconsin. Tom farmed 'em. His Holsteins were sleek and fat. His corn grew tall. His root house groaned with viands from season to season.

In addition to his success with the sandy soil Tom had added to his cash income by manufacturing in his barn a duck call. It was a lucrative business, even though the blamed duck call wasn't any good. It was further proof of the man's resourcefulness. In that country they say you can farm the sand "if you get three rains a week, but one of 'ems got to be fertilizer."

An optimistic settler with $10,000 and a pronounced deafness asked a friend what the prospects were on that soil for the growing of nuts. He thought he had received a favorable answer, bought land and went to work. In a few years he was broke. Accosting his advisor he complained:

"I thought you said I could grow nuts on that land."

"You got me wrong, neighbor. What I said was you'd GO nuts."

One more yarn before we return to Tom and the Big Pothole.

It's about the lumberjack who retired to a farm in the sand. He was a poor farmer. The 'jacks seldom made a success of farming after tasting the freedom of the camp, the drive and the town.

After a few years on his acres an old bunkhouse crony visited him. He noted a new settler nearby on land the 'jack had originally owned. The crony inquired about the new neighbor.

"Well sir," explained the 'jack, "the land was getting me down. I was looking for a buyer. This fellow came along and offered me $50 for 25 acres. But I fooled him! When I handed him the deed it was made out for 50 acres instead of 25!"

The President of the Old Duck Hunters and I had walked into the Big Pothole enough times to prove ourselves with Tom. You'd have thought he would relent and let us use his road but he declined to make any exception. Mister President, being on the resourceful side himself, tried various ways.

That is to say he tried everything but cold cash.

In the preamble to the Old Duck Hunters' constitution there is a word

about the Magna Carta, King John, that economic royalist, and the in-alienable rights of a gentleman in good standing to shoot the duck any place where he trespassed only upon the duck. Eminently fair. Bribes were all right, the President ruled. But no filthy lucre must change hands.

The bribes took the form of tailor-made cakes, cans of tobacco, and one or two bottles of the demon rum, of which at times Tom was inordinately fond, doubtless as solace for his stern struggle with the sand. These gifts were included in a five-year philanthropic progam at the end of which the association hadn't as much right to Tom's sacred road as the under sized chipmunks that ran up and down its ruts.

Personal relations between Tom and the association could not have been better. That was the galling part of it. Tom was an excellent neighbor — "Glad t' see ye, boys. Come right in and have a taste of Ma's new wine. Ain't seen hide nor hair of anyone but Ma in two weeks."

At such times the President would tactfully point out Tom could see the association much more often if he'd open up that road. That would send Tom into his shell. Anything but open the road. So the association continued to chafe its heels in rubber boots over the three-mile trail.

His duck calls were long black hollow affairs almost big enough for a rabbit to hide in. Perhaps he has never sold more than a few hundred of them at a dollar apiece but Tom is the kind of man who can make $200 go a long way. The President purchased his call from Tom in a weak moment when he thought Tom was going to let us drive in on his road. We had been warned that the call wasn't any good at all; that in fact the only good one he ever made he kept for himself!

This wonderful instrument, the local legend held, had a reed fashioned out of draw-filled copper. Or was it hand-hammered platinum? I do not recall. But after you once heard Tom employ it on a flock of cautious mallards, you were ready to believe it was a personal presentation from the angel Gabriel. No more accomplished Paganini of the marshes ever shook tobacco crumbs out of a duck call.

After a few blats from the commercial product which Tom had put on the market the President stowed it in his old brown mackinaw pocket and concluded:

"The old buzzard found the perfect formula and deliberately threw it away."

Came a morning late in the season when the Old Duck Hunters toiled over the three-mile trail by the aid of flash lights. It was pitch dark. Half

[82]

way in it began to snow and the going became slippery. The President was cussing Tom:

"If he'd let us use that road, we could have slept another hour this morning."

We scattered our eight decoys beyond the edge of the flaggers on the favorite west point, fixed up the bind a bit and settled back. Shooting time came and passed and Tom had not arrived. Though the snow was thick we would have heard him calling from any point on the pothole. His favorite blind, regardless of wind direction, was in what we called the south bay, a mere indentation in the shore. We were congratulating ourselves on Tom's absence when from the south bay became the unmistakable notes of Tom's tooter.

"He's just warming up to the day's work like a cornet player in a circus band," explained the President. "That's not his best. That's only 'Home Sweet Home' with one hand. Wait until he hits his stride on 'Auld Lang Syne' — two hands and triple-tonguing."

Through the snow we glimpsed a dozen mallards beating down the middle of the pothole. The President gave them a strident highball, his own vocal conception of "Yoo Hoo!" Hardly had he called and turned the mallards when Tom struck up his interpretation of a mallard come-all-ye on his duck call.

The mallards wheeled all the way around, disappeared in the snow headed for Tom's blind and shortly we heard two snow-muffled booms in the south bay.

"He's taking them right off our gun barrels!" the President snorted. "My call was a signal for him to begin. He didn't see those ducks through the snow. Man! That's grand larceny!"

The President's jaw projected outward a little. His brown eyes snapped. He laid the crooked little pipe carefully against a scrub oak bough and thrust a hand into the sagging pocket of the old brown mackinaw.

Forth came three old leg tethers for live decoys, reminders of better days, one plug of Brown's Mule chewing tobacco, slightly gnawed, four 20-gauge shells at which he sniffed contemptuously, and finally an object shiny and pocket-worn — the fraudulent instrument Tom had sold him for a duck call.

"Maybe I can get the damn thing to work," he muttered.

He peered through its barrel. He blew through it. Sand, tobacco crumbs, pocket lint and jack pine needles issued therefrom. But no sound.

[83]

The President probed the instrument with a long forefinger. But no matter how hard he blew he could not produce sound.

Finally he stepped from the blind and swished the instrument in the water. Something loosened up inside and the call did produce sound — "like a loon with a can tied to its tail," said the President. But it seemed better than nothing at the moment.

A pair of ducks were sighted. They saw our decoys, swung toward them. The President began what was intended as feeding chatter. The two mallards climbed like they had been shot. Almost instantly Tom, from his listening post, cut loose with his call. Again we waited. Again the two snow-muffled booms, significant witnesses to Tom's prowess with his magic tooter.

The President stood up and called upon his ancestors to witness that this was the foulest incivility ever visited upon an innocent man, "the work of a fiend incarnate." His Phillipic was moving. He made as though to fling Tom's spurious duck call into the pothole but stayed his arm when it was half way through the forward motion. The fire faded from his eyes and he grinned.

"The situation," he declared, "calls for that most sovereign of remedies, sweet oil and diplomacy. We've used up all our diplomacy but we've still got the sweet oil."

He fumbled in the other pocket of the old brown mackinaw. This time he produced a flat brown bottle which he uncorked and held to my nose — "If that isn't sweet oil, what is it?"

I said it smelled like applejack to me. I even mentioned that it had been my applejack and thought it had been in my pocket. The President explained I was right — "that's where it had been."

"It was originally confiscated out of sheer capitalistic greed," he explained, "but now I propose to — er — distribute it. Production for use is the term, I believe. Tom dearly loves applejack."

He left me. I watched him for a couple hundred yards before the snow swallowed him. It was obvious he proposed to inflict upon Tom the social amenity that the noble red man, late of these very acres, had found harder to cope with than cold and famine. Tom did like a dollop of rum and today was the day for it.

The President was absent an hour. From the east bay the boom of Tom's 12-gauge sounded less often. The President returned with the virtuous look of a householder who has gone outside in his night shirt on a stormy night to nail back a banging shutter.

'Tom,' he announced ungrammatically, 'is took care of — good!"

Three mallards loomed out of the snow. The Old Duck Hunters faded into the face of the blind. Suddenly from beside me came the noblest duck calling I had heard since Tom had been silenced. I turned my head to witness the performance. The President explained during a four bar rest that it wasn't Tom's. I was still laughing when I had waded back from the task of picking up two green heads.

"When I left Tom," said the President, "he was rolled up like a cocoon in his long sheepskin coat. Sound asleep. It's a caution what applejack will do on an empty stomach."

The President re-enacted the scene in the south bay blind. Tom had been his same old self. He'd been chilly when he heard a shell clink on glass in the President's pocket — "might chilly day. Ye ain't carryin' a drop are ye?" "Certainly, Tom, drink up. Now, about that road." No, Tom couldn't "go 'long on that. Say that's mighty perky hard cider. Well thanks, don't mind 'f I do." "If you ever change your mind about that road Tom, come and see me. Don't forget, Tom. I'll be waiting..." "Shure. Shure thing. Guess I'll take a little nap. Did'n sleep good las'h nigh'—."

It was then that the President of the Old Duck Hunters' Association had reached over and exchanged his spurious duck call for the real McCoy!

The real McCoy indeed. "It looks more like my old horn than my old horn does itself," said the President, studying it. "I'd take it apart and look at the reed but he seems to have it set just so. Anyway, if I can't make 'em I can play 'em."

He went to work with the stolen Stradivarius. When we saw ducks through the snow he invariably turned them. When none were flying within our limited range of vision the President practiced his repertoire, which is no limited portfolio. Just as good as Tom's, in fact. Give him an instrument the like of which he had that day and the result is pure art.

An hour passed. Finally from Tom's blind, following an especially loud highball by the President, came the sound of the President's late duck call. It was a ludicrous pip-squeak, thin and faked. It was followed by other attempts, each less like duck language than the previous.

"The old sinner," chortled the President. "That'll teach him. I'd give four of those greenheads we've got to be watching him right now."

During a silent interval from the south bay the President surmised that

[85]

Tom was taking it apart — "then he'll find out it isn't his own call. Ooop! Down — there's a pair!"

The Old Duck Hunters' Association was picking up its decoys when Tom showed up, as the President predicted he would. I was wrapping the cord around the mouth of the worn gunny sack after the pick-up. Looking up I saw Tom loom out of the snow, long sheepskin coat, ear-lapped hunting cap, high duck boots and all. His nap had served to restore him to a considerable extent. He was almost the same old Tom, cagey, courteous, sly, but a bit whiffy when you stood down wind from him.

He gossiped about the weather, the coming election, the high price of groceries and the outrageously low price of milk from the cow. We were on the point of leaving when he spoke up more to the point:

"Ye didn't see nothin' of an old duck tooter, did ye?"

"Can't say I did," the President replied.

"Funny, I lost mine some'eres. Certainly no one'd steal it..."

"Why, your tooter is hanging around your neck right now!" the President pointed.

"'Tain't mine," Tom said. "Mine's different."

"What do you mean different? I've got a tooter just like yours. You said you made one just as good as another. What difference does it make which one you've got?"

Tom colored. "Well, that ol' tooter was different," he said lamely.

"You don't mean to say you make some tooters better than others?"

"No, 'tain't that." Tom was floundering. "But you know how a feller gets t' feeling about his own tooter."

"Bosh!" the President snorted. "A duck call is a duck call. You stick the reed in a hollow wooden tube and there you are."

The President shouldered his gun and stretched out his hand — "We've got to run, Tom, if we're going to get back to town before the roads are snowed under."

"I was just thinkin'," Tom said. You could see he was, too. The President of the Old Duck Hunters had the pressure on him.

"I was just thinkin' that maybe next year I'd oughter let you fellers in by the road. It'd save work for ye."

"Splendid!" shouted the President. "Thank you so much. Now we must run. So-long, Tom. See you next fall."

The President turned again but Tom stopped him. Tom had never met a duck hunter as sharp as this before. His plight was growing desperate.

He'd given away his rights to the road and still hadn't got his duck call back.

"'Fore ye go," said Tom, "ye might look aroun' t' see if that ol' tooter of mine is about. I been shooting here during the week. Mebbe it's around..."

"Glad to help you look for it."

The President busied himself inside the blind and emerged triumphantly with the tooter. Tom seized it and satisfied himself with one gentle blast that it was indeed the tooter of the miraculous reed.

"This'n here," he said, removing the other from his neck cord, "is one I won't need any more. Be glad t' let ye have it."

"Will you guarantee it to work, Tom?" the President demanded.

Tom was himself again. He had his tooter back. There came into his eyes an old twinkle and this time I was positive he was grinning at us when he chortled:

"Guarantee it? I'll guarantee it to work just as good as your darned old applejack!"

*As one of the top outdoor writers of his time,
MacQuarrie in the course of his long career traveled
widely. There were few forms of hunting and
fishing and few of the famous areas unfamiliar to
him. Still, it is clear from these pages his first and
last love was the Wisconsin landscape, preferably
with his buddy at his side.*

*Enriching that landscape are the many people
with Scandanavian backgrounds. This is a tribute
to them, through gigantic Gus, all six feet four of
him. MacQuarrie's ancesters came from Scotland
but his relish in the delights of ethnic differences is
evidenced here. Obviously he took people as they
came without previous stamps. And he obviously
admired his chuckling giant, a man who could lose
a good fish with the best of them.*

Too Daggone White

In March, along the valley of Wisconsin's surging river Brule, there is a season, half spring and half winter, when ragged patches of snow linger at the feet of patient gray cedars, though the northering sun beats warmly in the tree-tops. Coffee-brown spew, stained from hemlock roots, oozes down the slopes to join the rising flow, and there is a great rushing of waters along the sixty-six miles of the Bois Brule. The old river is on the rampage from 'way up beyond Stone's Bridge clear to the mouth of Lake Superior.

It is a season when discontented fishermen peer petulantly out of windows, beyond dripping eaves, and wonder "if the rainbows are up." When that word is passed, all angling men of parts make haste to get to the river and inspect the annual miracle of 10- and 12-pound fish spawning almost at their feet.

On a windy, warmish-coldish March day 'long about tax-paying time I had occasion to pass the place of business of the President of the Old Duck Hunters' Association, Inc. Mister President was standing in his window with one I recognized immediately as Gus, six-foot-four Norwegian who can and does handle an 8-ounce fly rod as you and I handle one of half that weight. The President hailed me.

"The rainbows are up," he announced, and added hurriedly, "but I can't get down to see 'em till Sunday."

Gus had brought the tidings. He had just returned from the recently dismantled South Shore railway trestle which spans the famous creek

[89]

near a whistling post and switch block answering to the legendary Indian name of Winnebojou.

"They're up, all right," Gus affirmed. "By yingo, some dandies are laying on the gravel south of the trestle."

Only Gus didn't say it just like that. His Norse accent is something that cannot be reduced to paper. You can sort of play around with that accent, but you can't pin it down. You can give a fair imitation of the way of an Irishman with a word, or a Scotchman, or almost any other good American, but I have yet to see the speech of a Gus set down in black and white in a manner recognizable alike to those who know the Norwegians and the Norwegians themselves.

Suffice it to say that all the good, whole, sound, lusty and gusty Guses pronounce yellow with a "j" and January with a "y." There are other little nuances which this inadequate scribe can only hint at in print. But before we go farther, and to justify and glorify the Guses of this world, let all be advised that when they hear someone saying Yanuary instead of January they should listen closely, for that fellow is more than likely to know a lot about fishing.

There, in the President's garage, the chimes of memory started ringing in Gus' honest head. One thing led to another. Almost before we knew it, Gus was launched on a favorite tale. He began it in the little office of the President's establishment, but half-way through all hands moved into the more spacious showroom to give Gus elbow-room. Striding back and forth among the shining cars, Gus made that tale live and breathe.

Yentlemen, we give you Gus:

"There's just one bait to use in spring. What is it? Salmon eggs. Yudas Priest, what I could do down there today with one yar of salmon eggs and a Colorado spinner! Of course, it being illegal, you won't find me there, by yingo!

"You take a little spinner and throw away the hooks. Put on big bass hooks. Then, when you've got a fish, you've got him — yes-sir-ee. Anyhow, I was going to mention about that day down by the Dry Landing. It was opening day. Six thousand fishermen from Winnebojou down to McNeil's. I had two small ones, but they were — oh-h, about three pounds apiece, and I ain't going home opening day with sardines!

"There's a pretty good hole down there. I came up to it. Yudas! Sixteen fishermen and sixteen poles! Yiminy! I waited. They tried everything. Salmon eggs, spinners, worms, bucktails, streamers. I waited a good

hour, and they all left, one by one. Then I stepped in!"

Yentlemen, when Gus steps in, he steps into places where you and I would need a boat. There, in the showroom, we saw Gus easing himself out into the sacred pool, the water gurgling about his barrel chest.

"I knew that hole, all right," Gus continued. "I hadn't fished it twenty-five years for nothing. There I was. Out goes the first cast. All I had on was three salmon eggs with a spinner above. I let 'em slide down to the end of the hole where the water went faster. Nothing. Once again — "

All this was acted. Not just spoken. Gus strode from car to car. His huge feet thumped the showroom floor. His ruddy face grew ruddier with the zest of impending combat.

"Out I sent it again," Gus went on, eyes gleaming. "Down to the end of the hold. Then — oop! What's that now, eh? Comes on the spinner a little t-i-c-k! Um-hum. So he's there, eh? Umphum. Yaw. You wait, Mister Rainbow. Me and you are going to do business.

"Third time I cast out and felt the same t-i-c-k. I struck, and nothing happened. A wise one, that rainbow, stealing my salmon eggs. Strategy is what he needs. I put on new salmon eggs and cast again. T-i-c-k.

"Then I got bright idea. Instead of striking, I leaned over — "

When Gus leans over, it's like seeing the tower of Pisa tip farther.

"I leaned over and let 'em go down in there again — drift cast. I let 'em go two or three feet beyond where he was ticking it. I knew the fish would follow so as not to miss those salmon eggs. I hoped it would work, by yiminy."

You hope so too, as you listen, but you are pretty sure it will, because Gus has told you the tale a dozen times, and he tells it so well that people clear away furniture to hear it again and again in all its primal splendor. There is Gus, huge arms holding imaginary rod, chest-deep in the flow, swishing between the display automobiles. The air becomes tense. The moment is at hand.

"Just at the right time I felt the t-i-c-k. I knew he'd followed it down-stream. I knew he was turned in another direction. Right there I gave it to 'im and Yudas Priest — "

Gus almost went backward over a projecting bumper as he fought the big rainbow, but he got the trout into the open between two deluxe models and fought it out there, even to the point of standing proudly at the end of the fight, holding the flopping giant aloft in triumph.

Great people, those Guses of the northern parts of our lake states.

Where you find good fishing you'll find plenty of Norwegians and Swedes. They excel at the game, either as commercial or sport fishermen. They are anglers from the word go, and tough as all-get-out. The kind of lads the Big Ten coaches smile at when they report in September for the football team. Plenty of them have lugged the pigskin for Wisconsin and Minnesota, and plenty more of them will, by yiminy!

Gus is not only tall but proportioned. He used to fish with a pint-sized pal whom he carried through the deep holes on his back. Legend hath it Gus would stop from time to time and let his comrade whip the waters from this magnificent perch.

Gus departed. Mister President pulled out his watch. It was 2 P.M. He said: "If we jump in the car and run down there right now, the sun will be about right to see the big rainbows either off the South Shore trestle or from the front of the St. Paul Club."

"But I though — "

"Never mind thinking. My taxes are due tomorrow. My dandruff is bothering me. My chilblains are peeling, and besides I haven't been outdoors to speak of since last duck season. Come on!"

An hour and half later the President firmly fastened the single button of the old brown mackinaw and strode forth upon the creaking ties of the ancient trestle to be present at Act I, Scene I of "The Great Rainbow Drama," or "Why Life is Worth Living for Fishermen."

This first glimpse of the big lunkers from Lake Superior in the Brule is one of the Middle West's most dramatic and visible fish migrations. Smelt along the Lake Michigan shores provide another spectacle. Still another is that amazing run of wall-eyed pike up the Wolf River of Wisconsin from Lake Winnebago in April. You can see those newly arrived rainbows as they come up, whereas the smelt only run at night and the walleyes are deep goers. Hence the charm of this Brule spectacle. I have seen at one time as many as fifty persons staring down into the Brule, forty feet beneath them, from that old South Shore trestle.

You first see the fish as mere wavering shadows. The eye becomes adjusted to the riffle, and from a vantage-point you begin to get their outlines in detail. But the "ohs!" and "ahs!" are reserved for the moment when a big, crimson-streaked female rolls on her side and vibrates from stem to stern, apparently hastening the ejection of eggs. Then the startling color of the fish is plainly visible, after which the fish resumes its equilibrium and once more becomes a wavering shadow.

Of course, no fishing is permitted then. Fishing for those big fellows that sometimes lie by the score in a space no bigger than a large room would be sheer murder. Poachers, netters and spearers once reaped a bountiful harvest from the Brule, but vigilantes from game clubs, working with alert wardens, now keep nightly springtime watchers along the stream. One violator got in so deep that he spent a year in the state prison, perhaps as severe a penalty for a game-law violation as Wisconsin has ever seen.

The rainbow run up the Brule is something more than a movement of a splendid game fish. Poems have been written about it. People come from several hundred miles before the season opens to see the big fellows. Natives know it as a sure sign of spring.

This is related so that you may know what sort of pilgrimage called the President from his daily chores at tax-paying time. Right there on the old trestle the season opened for the Old Duck Hunters' Association. Thus it has begun for thousands of north country anglers. It is not for us here, to record the dragging days thereafter, nor the disorderly heaps of tackle laid out for overhauling, nor the endless remembering and the hopeful boastings that ensued between that day and the chill bright dawn of May 1, when the season opened.

It need be reported only that the Old Duck Hunters were there on time, a delicate achievement in itself, made possible by adjusting the get-away with precise calculation of sunrise time and allowing just so many minutes for breakfast, packing and deep prayer. The only delay occurred when the Association halted for a few minutes on a sticky clay road and helped push one of the brethren from a frost boil that had shattered the road's center. That accomplished, no less than thirty cars plunged swiftly through the wallow, labored out the other side and sped off Bruleward. You've got to see that opening-day assault upon the Brule to appreciate it.

There are places where you can escape the multitude, even on opening day. You can, for instance, go in by canoe on the fifteen miles of water from Stone's Bridge to Winnebojou and not see anyone for miles. But because it is canoe water and somewhat inaccessible, by far the great majority prefers to answer the roll call of the faithful in waders. The President voted against a canoe, and we parked with a hundred other cars in a Winnebojou clearing not far from the old trestle. It was Mister President's idea to elbow right in — "Let's try it and have some fun."

The report must be submitted that it was not a great deal of fun at that particular place. One reach of river perhaps a hundred yards long was accommodating twenty or thirty fishermen. Up-stream the concourse of fishermen diminished, but it was bad enough. These gatherings do produce fun, however. Everyone knew everyone else, and those who did not soon got acquainted. In such a crowd someone is bound to hook a good one or two, but the Old Duck Hunters emerged from the stream at noon with nothing to show for their labor and planning.

On the sunny side of a twisted cedar the President spread sandwiches, uncorked hot coffee and held council. Halfway through the third sandwich, when I was suggesting we forget the big fellows and go after some fun and small ones on the upper reaches, the President looked up suddenly with more than casual interest.

"On yonder well-worn fisherman's trail," he said, "comes the answer to our problems."

It was Gus. But he was despondent. Even three cups of coffee, which he drank scalding and straight, and liberal applications of sandwiches did nothing to cheer him. He said he had been "all over dis har river" since sunup. First near the mouth, then at Teeportens, down by Judge Lenroot's and at four or five other places. " — and there's a fisherman on every hold between here and Lake Superior, by yingo!"

Had he seen any good ones? He had, indeed. John Ziegler had one close to ten pounds. Carl Tarsrud had two of them, maybe five and six pounds. Clarence Grace hadn't done so badly. All are sure-fire Brule fishermen. Gus said he had seen maybe fifty rainbows of five pounds or over, "but by yiminy, I can't find a hole that hasn't been tramped."

He said he was quitting; that he would come back the following day, when the opening-day crew had departed. It is a fact that this opening-day rush on the Brule fades to practically nothing within a day or two. No Wisconsin stream can match it for the first day. We think the boys like to make a ceremony of it, and then go their many ways on hundreds of miles of other good streams all over the northern end of the state.

Gus was no sooner out of sight when the President swept the luncheon remnants together, grabbed at gear and with his mouth still stuffed urged: "We're following that boy. Hurry! I saw his car over in the grove a minute ago."

No fool, the Hon. President. He explained while we skulked along the trail, trying to appear unhurried, that Gus never in his life quit a stream until it was too dark to fish; that wherever Gus was heading now would be all right with us. And furthermore, that following Gus was perfectly legitimate, as also was Gus' attempt to veil his real intent.

All honest fishermen will understand the code. You get what you're good enough to take, with due consideration for bag limits, the folks you are dealing with and your own immortal honor. We watched Gus back out his car and followed along unobserved on a county trunk running parallel to the river.

In the town of Brule, rainbow-trout capital of Wisconsin, where the famous from Presidents Cleveland through Coolidge and Hoover have passed, Gus halted his throbbing engine long enough to clump into Hank Denny's restaurant. From the bulge of his lower lip when he reappeared, we guessed he had laid in a new stock of "snoose." Or snuff, if you are unfamiliar with this tidbit. Or, if you are familiar with it, "Norwegian dynamite."

It was easy to trail Gus because of the heavy traffic. He passed the road into the old Banks place and the one down to the N. P. Johnson bridge. We thought he might have turned at these places with the idea of hanging around until fishermen had quit certain holes. But Gus had another spot in mind.

Traffic thinned, and Gus turned left, down a road that we knew well. A road not too safe at that season of frost boils, when red clay seethes and softens.

Gus must have known it was a long shot he was taking. No one else had braved that road during the day. It was ticklish work. You slide down one hogback and bluff your way up the next, wheels flinging red-clay chunks twenty feet high into the popple trees. At the bottom of a steep hill we found Gus mired.

We climbed out. We gave aid. We spoke frankly of our intentions. Gus laughed. Gus always laughs. With me driving and Gus pushing, we made the hill with both cars, slid down the next descent, and there we were, practically on the bank of the Brule.

"Vell," said Gus, chuckling, as we surveyed the river, "I don't know but what it serves me right to sneak away from you and get stuck."

The Brule at this point, only a few miles from the big lake, was yellowed with red clay washed down from eroding banks that stretch along the river some distance back from its mouth. Gus remarked that a trout could use a pair of glasses to advantage. Murky water has never bothered the

President much. He holds it gives an angler an advantage, permitting him to work water more searchingly without frightening fish. All things considered, he'll take a roily creek to one gin-clear, and he's not entirely a bait fisherman, either. In its upper reaches, by the way, the Brule runs gin-clear the year round.

The place where we put in is below what is known as McNeil's Hole. The McNeil farm lies along the Brule bottoms. Below a bridge at this point the river bends sharply to the east, then turns again straight north and before caroming off a high bank to the west idles awhile in a long, deep hold.

The Old Duck Hunters love that place. The biggest steelhead I ever saw actually taken from the river came out of that hole on the end of Mister President's leader. It was a seven-pounder. And I mean steelhead, a fish identified carefully later by E. M. Lambert, superintendent of the fabulous Pierce estate upstream.

Lambert knows a steelhead from a rainbow. But he cannot tell at a glance, and neither can anyone else. All you can do is guess. The steelhead is likely to be whiter, but beyond that the boys who know go into the matter by counting scales. However, this is no place to discuss that. There was work at hand.

I went up-stream and worked down under the bridge and around the corner with salmon eggs and a spinner. No fun? Well, yentlemen, as Gus would say, "There are times when the water is too damn wet for dry flies!"

I creeled a few small rainbows and worked toward the big pool which Gus and the President had fished. The latter had a nice four-pound rainbow — a dark, deep-bodied, typical Brule rainbow with a pronounced crimson sash down his side. Gus was out there waist-deep, working everything in his catalogue for another he had seen "roll like a poorpuss, by yiminy."

"He was white as a ghost," Gus yelled at me from midstream. "Maybe I can get him."

The Old Duck Hunters watched the show. It is always a show to watch Gus. He can wade almost any place on the Brule. That rugged river holds no terrors for him. His powerful legs stand against its brawling push where other legs would wabble and shake. He was using his best formula: salmon eggs and spinner.

You who have not fished the Brule, you who have only read about it,

[97]

should see it with one like Gus performing in its center. It was getting on toward late afternoon. The warmth of the May sun was being dissipated by the familiar chill that rises from the Brule on the hottest days. Gus stood in almost five feet of water, the yellow flow nipping his wader tops. He nursed the "snoose" in his lower lip and practiced his art.

I saw the fish roll once to the spinner. It was indeed stark white, as Gus had said. A good sign to the layman that it was a true steelhead. The Old Duck Hunters smoked and watched, conscious of imminent drama. Finally it happened.

Gus' rod arm went forward and down — he hooks 'em that way. Then the arm was back up and throbbing, and something hard and white and crazy exploded from the pool, forty feet away. Gus backed toward shallow water. The big white fish ran up-stream and leaped many times. They will do it before you can think. From the pool came a snoose-muffled roar, such a one as Gus' Viking ancestors might have bellowed in a foray on the Irish coast a thousand years ago.

"Yudas! I got 'im!" he snorted.

To which the President of the Old Duck Hunters added fervently, "Yiminy whiskers, Gus, give 'im snoose!"

Snoose it was in the first, second and third degrees. Of the battle, of the raging to and for, of the unbelievable strength in six pounds of fresh-run steelhead, of the great grunts and snorts from Gus, there is little need for setting down. Suffice it to say the fish took Gus down-stream fifty yards, came back into the pool and dogged and bucked and leaped and writhed and rolled on the leader until he was washed up.

All these things have been reported many times. No fish in Wisconsin will exhibit the electric insanity of a hooked steelhead in fast water.

After about twenty minutes there was the ghost-white fish on the tiny shelving sand beach at the edge of the pool, and there were two grand old fishermen shaking hands, and there was an ancient gunny sack extracted from Gus' jacket. Into this the big fish went. The mightiest of Wisconsin trout rivers had once more flashed its beaming smile upon the Old Duck Hunters, Inc.

Indeed, it was a chalky fish. Along the lateral line there was hardly more than the faintest wash of crimson. You looked closely to see it. All the rest of him was white, bluish in places, but white — the sign of the steelhead. A sign we could check later with Emmett Lambert, the Brule's grand old authority, if we so desired. Lambert could take measurements and say what he was. For the present there was only supreme content among the Old Duck Hunters.

Gus dipped a blunt forefinger into the round box and spread a damp layer of snoose under a quivering lower lip. It is something to see a six-foot-four Norwegian trembling. Fact is, we were all trembling. And you will, too, if you ever come to grips with one of those Lake Superior submarines. The President got out his omnipresent thermos bottles and passed around hot coffee. His own rainbow, a nice little fish, was forgotten for the larger one.

A native with a long cane pole and a sad look wended toward us from McNeil's bridge. To his hail, "Anything doing?" gus extracted the still-writhing steelhead from the sack and held it high over his head by its lower jaws. The native's eyes popped. He was about to say something when the steelhead contorted in a quick spasm, wrenched free and dropped into the pool.

Gus lumbered toward the fish, scooping desperately. The fish rolled and slithered out of his grasp, and then, with new strength, shot like a torpedo for deep water.

No one spoke for perhaps a half minute. The President's coffee spilled from its cup. I shall never forget the gone feeling that hit me. The native seemed sadder than ever. All eyes were on Gus. For only an instant his face was tragic. Then he grinned. A grin that wrinkled and spread and warmed his great red face and lighted it with something you seldom see on the face of a man in such extremity.

He spoke: "Well, boys, he was a pretty good fish. But damn it, I didn't like his color. He was too dog-gone white!"

Too-dog-gone white! That from a fisherman who had felt his heart turn a handspring in his throat. Do you wonder why I love those Norse fishermen?

Yentlemen, this reporter begs a last line: When all the fishing is over for Gus, when he will no longer hear the kingfishers screaming along the stream, when all that remains of him is a magnificent legend of a great-hearted fisherman, the Old Duck Hunters will write an epitaph for Gus, and this is what it will be:

"Too dog-gone white."

Now we meet another of MacQuarrie's great loves — his cabin.

While he was still in his teens his father, a carpenter, built a log cabin on one of the Eau Claire chain of lakes. In those days right after the first World War, it was a 16 mile walk into it from the nearest railroad stop. Later, of course, roads cut through the woods and it was reachable by auto.

The cabin, doubtlessly improved over the years was the author's heart of hearts. It figures in one story after another, an enviable place, a romantic spot on the edge of the lake, with chipmunks and whiskey jacks for neighbors, a story book headquarters for any hunter and fisherman.

Canvasback Comeback

It was a bad night for driving north and west through Wisconsin. Beyond the windshield, through stabbing sleet and snow, the President of the Old Duck Hunters' Association waited. So I kept a-going.

Mister President would be draped before an open fire. He'd be wearing the worn gray carpet-slippers and the sweater vest with the bulged lower pockets where he stuck his thumbs. Outside the cedar-planked cabin the storm would be hammering while he dozed.

I was ninety miles from this happy rendezvous, tooling a car through a storm that was making seasonal history, and making Mister President's duck-hunter soul gladder by the minute. I should have known better than to delay the start-off. But at 6 P.M. it is too late to do anything about that sort of thing. The only possible course was to blast on through. The President was waiting up.

Near Loretta-Draper, Wisconsin, I stopped at Flambeau Louie Johnson's and in twenty minutes (a) consumed a warm meal, (b) heard once more of my shortcomings because I had failed to land that 40-pound muskie last summer, and (c) promised Edie Johnson on my honor I'd take it slow and easy up that fire-lane road. Those two good friends came to the door to look anxiously after me as the car surged up the hill into the storm, heading for Highway 70, the fire lane, Clam Lake, Cable, Drummond — and the Middle Eau Claire Lake of Bayfield County, where Hizzoner smoked and dozed and waited.

[101]

There was new warmth in me when I left. All of it was not from Edie Johnson's superfine Scandinavian coffee, either. It was an inward warmth engendered by the certain knowledge that two good people would have restrained me by force if they had thought they could get away with it. Truth is, I enjoyed that drive. Revived by food, I had just one thing in mind — the sudden flood of light on the little cabin stoop when Mister President swung open the door at the sound of my motor.

That trip had some fierce and splendid moments. The fire lane straight north from Loretta-Draper is no playground for a hard-road driver. It demands a man of the Model T vintage, inured to highway trickery and the feel in the seat of the pants that prevents skids. The fire lane, now open to all, penetrates the wildest country I know in Wisconsin. There are no houses by the wayside to fall back on. You push up in there and take your own chances.

I felt my way at a cautious 20 per. It grew colder. Thank heaven, I know that fire lane. I know where the quick, sharp turns lie in wait for the reckless driver, where the narrow little bridges are, and where a man has to take the snowy hills in a steady-pulling second gear to save himself from sliding backward into a ditch.

Big trees went down in that night's wind. Afterward the wildlife experts said the blow leveled enough white cedar to take care of north Wisconsin's overgrown deer herd through the ensuing winter. It was fun. I love storms and lonely roads.

Twice I got out and whaled away with an ax to clear the road. On the twisting north end of the fire lane, slogging toward Cable, speed was cut to 15 miles per hour. What if I was late? Wasn't the Old Man waiting? Wasn't this blast just what the doctor ordered?

The plot was bluebills, maybe canvasbacks! It had been a long time since the Old Duck Hunters had hung a bag of cans. The scene was to be the broad, shallow south end of the Middle Eau Claire Lake, which the natives call Libby Bay. The scenario had been written weeks in advance by Mister President, who is a genius at guessing what weather does to duck flights. He was to be there with the necessary equipment, and I was to drive in on him.

It required three hours to make Cable, a journey ordinarily achieved in half that time. The town was asleep in the storm. I didn't have the heart to wake up the McKinneys and demand more coffee. But the worst was over. The treacherous fire lane was behind me. The snow was deepening, but I was now on black-topped Highway 63. The road was strewn with limbs torn off and hurled willy-nilly. A few of them had to be thrown aside. Others I just drove around.

When I made the left turn to the west at Drummond, the snow was six inches deep and still coming. No more sleet now. Just snow. That kind of snow can't last in this country on that kind of wind. The wind was north and west, a cold-wave wind. A bad snow wind here would have to be from the northeast. It was very cold. I could feel the sharper air working through the car doors, and turned the heater up to full blast.

The roadside trees at my turn-in were carrying terrific burdens. The brittle jack-pines were hard hit, many of them broken and hundreds of them bent so badly by wet snow that they have never recovered, but continue to thrive in the tenacious way of the fire pine at odd, sharp angles.

I parked the car at the hilltop as a precaution against having to buck snow uphill later, grabbed a duffel bag and a shotgun and plowed toward the lighted windows. It was late: so there was no good reason why Hizzoner should be up. The anticipated challenge from the stoop was not realized, but as I came up the picture was still a proper one for a conclave of the Old Duck Hunters.

Through the door window I saw Hizzoner dozing in the big chair before the open fire — just as he should have been. Sure enough, he wore the old gray sweater vest and the worn gray slippers. The little crooked pipe had fallen from his hand and lay beside him on the floor. Flames from the fire threw shadows against the warm cedar walls and ceiling.

I stepped from icy cold into peaceful warmth, stamped my feet and heard the verdict as he leaped up: "I knew you'd be damfool enough to try it? Do you realize this is the worst November blow to hit this country since 1930?"

He fumed. Didn't I know that main highways were blocked with drifted snow and deadfalls? Didn't I know that by morning it would be as cold as a monkey in Iceland? Didn't I know that the thermometer was 20, and dropping?

"Your Honor," I pleaded, embracing his lean, hard shoulder, "shut up and pour me a cup of coffee."

He lost no time. Before I had gear assorted, the rich aroma filled the kitchen and the big living room. With the coffee was half a breast of duck and a batch of biscuits, the like of which Mister President can whip up while efficient lady cooks of this generation are pouring through a cook book for a recipe.

The duck was a big fellow. The breast was big as a mallard's, but it was not a mallard.

"Canvasback," explained Mister President. "Straight from heaven knows where. They've been plumping into Libby Bay like they never have in ten years. Canvasback..." There was adulation in his voice, "Canvasback...I've been living on 'em since I came, four days ago. They slid in ahead of this blow. They've got Libby Bay plastered with floating celery they've dug up. They come to the bay in the morning, fill up and haul back to the quieter pot-holes. Canvasback..."

No finer tribute was ever paid the long-faced can than the gleam in Mister President's eye that late, stormy night.

He drove me to bed under the scarlet blankets. Then he asked, "You got enough shells for the both of us?" An old joke with him.

I said, "More'n enough," and barely caught his reply, "So you think," before drifting off as the wild wind screamed over the ridge pole.

The wind was still pouring it on when he switched on the light and held his little alarm clock a foot from my eyes. It read 4:30 A.M.

"Get up, you pup," he said firmly.

The snow had stopped. He predicted the wind would blow itself out during the day, but that we would have a mighty fast ride before it to the point blind by the Hole in the Wall.

In the blowy dark we went down the hill. He uncovered the motor, and I shoved off. One turn brought a volley that drowned out the roar in the tossing pines. By instinct and habit he cut the boat sharp from the shore and headed with the wind toward Libby Bay.

He was indeed right. Never had I had such a surging ride to the duck point which we call the Hole in the Wall. The wind was in complete charge. The lake shore, speeding past, was a mere dark line of trees on the broad white beach where snow was drifting deeply. Without that wind to churn the waters and prevent a freeze-up, we never would have got away from shore. As it was, the whole lake was open.

In pitch-dark against the lee shore he drove the boat into a scattering of shore willows. It was automatic with me to crawl over the prow, pull the nose up farther and lay hands on gear.

Mister President pulled on trout waders deliberately. He is no man to become hurried when the time nears and excitement grows. He holds that "with a little sweet oil and diplomacy a man can skin a cat alive." Never in

[104]

his mature life has he tossed a hurried set-up of boosters on the waters, then leaped into the blind to sit and hope. When he gets through, they are spread correctly.

He laid them in the formation which he has learned is best for the deep divers, a semi-horseshoe of decoys with the bulk of them at the toe of the shoe and a long lead line of decoys running straight out to form one long arm of the shoe, parallel to the direction of the wind. It was coming daylight when he had completed this careful rite. He joined me in the blind, pulled off the waders for more freedom and worked three shells into his automatic. As yet there was no light for seeing. We could make out the far shore of Libby Bay, but that was about all. We could hear the waves bickering in front of us and the pines moaning behind us. It was a fine morning.

Daylight was stubborn. It came tentatively over the far eastern shore of Libby Bay. But it did not like what it saw. It hesitated, then grudgingly conceded itself a victim to the turning of the spheres, and Mister President said, "Look!"

He needn't have said it. I had been trying to decide if that black mass in midbay was ducks or jut some quirk of the eerie morning light on tossing water. It would be there, and it wouldn't be there. One minute it would be ducks. Then it would be gray light and gray waves.

"They'd rather stay in the pot-holes, but they can't resist that celery," he whispered.

All seasoned blindsmen whisper when they smell the smoke of battle. It was just habit with him, although the ducks couldn't have heard him if he had yelled through a megaphone.

The first shock troops rode over us from behind on the screaming wind. They were not seen until they had almost taken off our hats and were far beyond the decoys. No use in listening for wings on such a morning. It was eyes or nothing.

"They spent the night on the thoroughfare, and came straight from it, hungry as wolves," Mister President guessed.

Our Hole in the Wall is a 40-acre backset off Libby Bay proper, with one good blunt-nosed point. It is a fine place when the wind is right. This morning the wind was perfect — right at our backs.

The first fair targets came like fighter planes spang into the wind; blazing through the Hole in the Wall for quieter waters, which they can find hereabouts in hundreds of pot-holes and many rivers and creeks. The

[105]

performance was instinctive with the Old Duck Hunters. He took his side, and I took mine. those low incomers on a 35-mile blast are not missed often. Not canvasback!

"Five," he remarked as they drifted off in the waves. "One for you and four for me."

I know full well that two of them were mine. But he insisted he nailed three with his first two shots, and then picked a crossing shot with his final shell. Who am I to quarrel with the leader of the Old Duck Hunters?

All were canvasback, and mighty welcome visitors to these waters which their ancestors had used for thousands of years. Welcome indeed! Northern canvasback, broad in the bill and broad in the breast. Just the kind of canvasback a man should be collecting here so late in the season.

The lake was completely ours. Not another hunter was around. The thermometer was around 10 above. Our blind protected us well, as do all late-season blinds fashioned by Hizzoner. He had even built a low wooden bench which was propped against the back wall. He sat there on the bench, a grand old patriarch in the storm. Beneath the rim of his shapeless brown hat there was white to match the snow in the dented hat crown. And in the furrowed collar of the old brown mackinaw there was more white, where the snow lit and stuck.

Sixty years old. And it was 10 above, with a wind...A drop stood on the end of his nose. A happy light gleamed in the sharp brown eyes. There was an alertness about him, as indicated by the quick right hand, ever ready to shake off the scuffed leather mitt.

Often have I looked at him in blinds such as this. From the smooth-bottomed rubber larrigans to the top of the ancient brown hat there was character. Character smelted and shaped by hard work, many worries and a dominant determination to be a decent human being.

He was aglow that morning; he was a part of the morning. I have seen him equally excited at the first arbutus on the chill forest floor of April. I have seen him so while fighting a good fish, still-hunting a buck, or planting a pine tree.

"The natives think the season is over," he gloated. "They think everything's gone through."

Hurtling flocks of bluebills tore loose from the rafted birds, and after the first few bunches had dusted across the decoys it was no longer necessary for the President to lay a warning hand on my knee. He was out for canvasback, to show me a come-back bag limit on a precious species which has made prodigious gains these past few years.

The big graybacks kept coming. In that kind of shooting a man can cultivate a careless rhythm to his swing. No need to stiffen. Almost every bird was centered. Such plentitude insures that most important conditioning factor of wing-shooting — relaxation.

At the noon hour Oscar fought across in his outboard from the far side of the bay to investigate the shooting at the Hole in the Wall. Oscar is a trapper of remarkable skill, a man who knows where otter play, yet refuses to trap them. He is a man who might some day stumble on to the last wolverine in Wisconsin. It would be a rare remnant of a species. He is fairly sure there is one of them in the wilderness of the near-by Totogatic country.

No duck hunter, Oscar. Rather is he a pack-sack and gum-boot man of the purest ray serene. He sat between us on the bench for an hour, ate a sandwich and munched an apple. Twice he borrowed the Old Man's automatic and took his share of the birds using his watery front yard for a restaurant.

When he departed in the afternoon, he hardly had to turn over the motor or touch the tiller, except to steer. Once beyond the quiet water inshore, his sturdy skiff was picked up and blown across the bay to his own far point.

"She'll die out by sundown," Mister President opined. "Can't blow longer. The wind is getting tired."

"I'd better walk around the shore and pick 'em up while there's still daylight," I suggested.

"The boat'll be easier — quicker."

But I wanted to stretch legs and set out, despite his warning that it would be a good four miles coming and going. Back among the shore pines and stripped of the heavy hunting jacket, I fought through six to eight inches of snow, concealed down-stuff and whipping brush.

First, the long way around the Hole in the Wall. Then up the sharp hill, panting, where I could look across water and down upon the lone, patient figure in the snowy blind. I went through the popple blow-down to the pine stand and the place where we drag up the boat to boil a dish of tea on good bass days. And so around through low tamarack country to the east side of Libby Bay. The waves had thrown every duck up on the beach. Some had been tossed on their backs by the waves, so that they stood out starkly.

They were a load. I was glad I had shed the heavy hunting jacket, and glad my boots had good treads on the bottoms, so that they gave me footing in the snow. An extra rawhide boot-lace saved the day. By tying the ducks together with it I could tote them with fair comfort.

As I came up in back of the blind, pretty tired, I saw the perfect finish. A single canvasback laced through the Hole in the Wall. The President waited until the duck was well over the land before firing, and then dropped it neatly far back of the blind, where I picked it up.

True to his prediction, the wind faltered at pick-up time. When we headed back, it was gusty, but the determined strength was out of the storm. The clouds were growing ragged. Before we made shore on the long run there were a few stars visible. A still, cold night coming up, he forecast.

The fireplace ashes were harboring coals. I brought them alive with birch bark and pine knots. Welcome heat surged through the big room. Mister President set the thermometer out on a jack-pine, and said it was crowding zero already. The stars were blazing and beautiful.

"How come," I said over the last cup of coffee, "you took a chance on that last bird? We might have had a limit already, you know."

"I counted 'em."

"But it might have been darned easy to count 'em wrong."

He was weary now. Five days of early rising were showing up on the peerless leader of the Old Duck Hunters. The reaction was setting in. Nodding a bit, he said: "I allus make allowances. A limit apiece — on canvasback."

"You sure hit it right. You shot half of 'em, and I shot half of 'em."

The warm room felt awfully good to him. He was almost asleep in the big chair, but declined to come full awake and challenge me. He just grinned, eyes half closed and said, "Oh sure...sure."

*The years have been marching on. It is now
1942 and the nation was into the savage struggle
of World War II.*

*But the war is far away from the bluebills coming
in over the Norways on the high hill beyond with
every foot on the throttle. "Great imagery here,"
wrote one editor on this project. "Not the best
story but perhaps his best writing. Concise."*

*As you read it, look for one wasted word. If you
find one, sent it to me and I'll have it mounted.*

High Hill Pothole

Most of the lakes were frozen. You know how that is. You hope they will stay open for another week-end, but the man out there phones with the dismal news and you retire the bags of decoys to the basement.

The President of the Old Duck Hunters' Association, Inc., felt as badly about it as I did. We were returning from social business with our wives through beloved duck country. We were pretty glum. It's tough to see the lakes in north Wisconsin glaze up hard in mid-November.

Our car just about knew its own way through the frozen barren-lands trails. The respective ladies occupied the back seat. The Old Duck Hunters held forth sadly in the front seat. Lake after lake was passed as Mister President spun the wheel this way and that. All of them were alike — still, frozen, dead.

He was getting sadder by the minute. Like the respectful satellite that I am, I reflected his mood. The supreme court in the back did not even look out the window when Hizzoner, suddenly inspired, turned sharp right and sent the car down a narrower sand trail. I knew where he was going.

"It's frozen like the rest," I said.

"We'll see," he grunted.

He was heading, of course, for Robinson Lake, one of the 6,138 known, named lakes in Wisconsin. I felt it was a waste of rubber, getting us off our homeward beat about five miles. On a little rise in the road he slowed down and studied Robinson's surface through the scrub at his right. Sure enough, it was frozen. Just like I had said.

He eased a foot down on the brakes to give himself a sure, passing glance at Robinson's deep end. Protests were heard from the rear. They had begun to sense what might happen. Suddenly he set the brakes hard and cranked down his window. And then he was out of the car, overcoat flapping, smashing through the brushy shore-line to get an unobstructed view. I followed.

Together we stood beyond the last fringe of jack-pine on Robinson's broad sand beach, and there, before us, were about a thousand bluebills, diving and chuckling and making a great fuss in the wide, open, deep end. Cheerful, sturdy rascals, those bluebills. A freak temperature drop to five above zero had not pushed these stout birds south. How do they find the few open lakes after such a freeze-up? And in such numbers? I was wondering about that and thinking about Bryant's "To a Waterfowl" as Mister President ripped off his spectacles and snorted: "Darned if I can see a rod through these cheaters! You got a clean handkerchief?"

After he had polished vigorously he studied the tardy congress out there with professional discernment. He asked me how many I thought were there. That was a presidential trap which I avoided. I said five hundred, though I knew a thousand was the minimum.

But if I had said quickly, without thinking, that there were five thousand, the old boy would have snorted his contempt and declared: "No such a thing! There are not over a thousand of them!"

It saddened him to find me bulletproof to one of his whimsies, but he took the next best tack. He said, "Mister, you and me are going hunting in the morning."

May I here be permitted to draw the curtain upon the scene back at the car. All I can admit for the record is that both Hizzoner and myself had been away from home practically all of that duck season. Boys, it was tough!

The red November dusk in which we drove home would have been one of nature's triumphs had it not been for my own dear lady, whose words still ring in these frost-bitten ears: "The fool expects to hunt in the morning, and the coal man dropped four tons of coal on his decoy bags yesterday. Ha, ha!"

Verily, they'll say it every time.

It was my own fault for storing them in the coal bin. It hurt to learn that two dozen of the best lamp-blacked bluebill decoys extant were immured beneath 8,000 pounds of coal.

For the first and last time in my life, I shoveled coal that evening preparatory to going duck hunting. I shoveled coal. And she sat on the basement step and swore, by every shovelful, that I was crazy as a loon. She said that I was as crazy as her father, which is one of the finest compliments ever paid me. Her father is President of the Old Duck Hunters.

As I shoveled I thought of Robinson Lake and its crinkly sand shore. I thought of the drooping red sun in the clear cold Wisconsin sky, of the way the black pines huddled on the distant shore-line, and of the animated scene in the open water where the bluebills fed and played. Such thoughts are a powerful help to a weary coal shoveler.

Mister President arrived for an inspection just as I was dusting off the second sack of decoys. His daughter was for giving him battle, on general principles, but all he was interested in was the condition of the wooden necks on the decoys after that coal disaster.

"You fixed?" he asked.

"I'll be waiting for you at 2:30."

"Give me a bag of decoys now. Get the heavy stuff out of the way. Don't bother to brush your teeth after I honk..."

I slept on the davenport downstairs so as not to disturb the civilized folks in my household.

His honk by the curb found me ready, of course. We satellites of the Old Duck Hunters are either ready, or we just don't go again.

Actually, there is only one sound and quick way to get acquainted with the outdoors: go find the old-timer. That is the road with the fewest chuck holes.

"Good morning, pup," he said, a greeting that was both a salute for being young and a reproach for not knowing much.

He leaned over the steering wheel. The glow from the instrument board highlighted his strong, brown face. He was as alive at that unseemly hour as it is given to few men to be alive. And the reporter must record that his daughter never saw the morning she got out of bed without singing, or maybe whistling.

As he drove he had me fill the crooked little pipe, and its ruddy glow cast another highlight on his face. We sped through the dark.

"You aiming to hunt Robinson?"

The query brought a tolerant glance. "Maybe," he said, "I know a place."

That was enough for me. The first rule for getting on with Mister President is to ask questions and settle for any answers you can get. By all means ask the questions, but never, never establish issues. It's like arguing with a lumberjack about the difference between a cant-hook and a peavey.

The fact is that I have seen Mister President wipe out an argument with nothing more complex than a grin. Once I watched him listen studiedly to a loud-mouthed gentleman who was in a great dither. When the gent ran out of steam, Mister President laid a brotherly hand on his shoulder and said, "George, don't be a jackass." George never did get to be one, either.

Hizzoner turned the wheel over hard and sent the car tunneling through scrub-oak and jack-pine. Then I knew where we were going. We were going to a place that has no name so far as I know. To be sure, the President refers to it as "the high hill pot-hole," but that would hardly do for the Geological Survey.

It is a lake somewhat less than a half mile long, half as wide and very deep for its size. Wisconsin is littered with the like. Its fish are mostly under-sized largemouth bass. It offers no feed for the tip-up ducks whatever. But in the late season Hizzoner refers to it as "the best bluebill washroom in fifty miles."

Lakes like this, spring-fed and wide open, are merely one of those legitimately marked cards held up the sleeve for emergencies. He eased the car down a steep sand trail, jammed it into scratchy cover and went into action.

"Grab those decoys! Hand me the shell-cases! Listen!"

With arms full of gear, I listened. From out on that pot-hole came the ancient music of the bluebills. It was dark as pitch. I stumbled in getting down the last of the hill. Mister President's smooth-worn rubber boots remembered the path well.

No quick blind for us! Nothing nervous or makeshift about the pit which had been dug in the sandy shore. True, day was breaking, but Hizzoner likes thoroughness. I have seen him build 'em with ducks overhead and in range. That is all a part of his philosophy.

An owl hooted beyond the Norways across the pot-hole. A smudge of gray grew in the east. The upper air was slit with wings. In that enchanting dawn-light of a surly November day the Old Duck Hunters began the grand old ritual.

[115]

"You sure you've got enough shells for the both of us?" he whispered. For answer I opened my crammed shell-box.

True to form, he snorted, "Will you ever learn not to bang that shell-box?"

While I was groping for some juvenile retort he stood up, brushed aside a bit of blind and shot twice. On the leaden waters I saw two white-breasted bluebills drifting beyond the decoys. He turned his head away. I knew he was laughing. And why not? Perhaps some day it will be my turn to laugh at the next one. I hope it'll be as good.

His two shots set up a commotion in the pot-hole. A couple of hundred bluebills made spluttering take-offs. A dozen hustlers banked against the dim Norways on the high hill beyond and came over, every foot on the throttle. The President just crouched and grunted.

His complete intensity in a pinch has always fascinated me, as it did then. He caught them when they were far out, and he picked places that counted. Four more bluebills were in the waves afterward. I had not fired. He turned on me.

"It ain't," he said, "that you ain't been taught to do right."

"Your honor," I pleaded, "I just wanted to see if that grunting of yours helped."

"It depends," he snapped, "on who does the grunting."

In due course I had my chance. There was no hurry. No guns resounded from neighboring frozen lakes. The country was ours. Give a bluebill open water, and he will stay on. He is insulated against everything except lack of food. Collect a late-season bird, and mark the bulk of feathers on that broad breast.

The morning wore on. There was a sun somewhere behind that heavy sky, but it wasn't in earnest about the day. It didn't come out at all. It was so dark shortly after noon that Mister President said he would have to hurry home soon and bed down the stock.

Darkness came early. The northeast wind howled down from the high hill beyond with snow in its mouth. When the shawl collar of Mister President's brown mackinaw showed a white rim of unmelted flakes, I knew it was close to pick-up time.

The moist cold had reddened his cheeks. A lock of gray had escaped from beneath the brown hat. He made the decision: "There's enough bluebills on yonder shore for both. Go ahead and pick 'em up."

I walked around the shore, glad for a chance to warm up. Every duck was a fat, chunky bird, the kind that hit the Wisconsin lakes at the end of the season, full up with the fat of the land stretching north a thousand miles and more.

Returning, I saw a visitor at the blind. He was helping the President at the tricky job of retrieving the decoys without a boat. Just so quickly does the head of the Association win friends. They were chatting like old comrades when I got to the blind. He was a native. He had "been out around the country all day and never seen a bird."

Mister President chose two fat drakes and gave them to him. Then he explained me. "This here young feller is my assistant. I'm teaching him the ropes."

The new friend eyes his birds and grinned at Mister President.

"Looks to me like you're doin' a mighty good job of it," he said.

"You would like that place. It is a very special place"... where long slanting shafts of the sun daub the leafless popple with bland yellows and grays.

For a man to be able to transmit all the color and aura of the outdoors he must feel it himself deeply. MacQuarrie embraced it all. The migrating juncos. The deer prints in the sand. The conservation balance of the wisdom of experience against the scientists in the labs. The unique excitement of ruffed grouse.

And always the deeper conservation message of giving thanks for very little. A brace of grouse apiece. Who shall ask for more?

A Brace Apiece

The way to get at partridge is to get at 'em. This not-so-little bird with the metallic green shawl and the cute fan-tail has too long been identified with a leisurely sort of hunting where you prowl through delightful old orchards and wild-grape tangles, a nonchalant shotgun under the crook of your left arm and the smoke of Indian summer in your nostrils.

When we go partridge hunting, we take off our hunting jacket. We surrender its convenient, indispensable pockets for a light-weight shirt, one as impervious to thorns as our wardrobe affords. We step into a pair of equally thorn-proof pants and the lightest boots we own. We grab two handfuls of shells and a piece of cord for tying Old Ruff to our belt, in lieu of that convenient, indispensable hunting jacket, which sometimes makes us sweat.

Let no man say *Bonasa umbellus* has not fanned our spark of appreciation. Let no man suspect this regal flyer has not caught our fancy for his grace. And for his poetry, too, dammit. It's just that hunting him and thinking about him are two different things.

Thinking about him is something else. In retrospect it is strictly cricket to hark fondly back to the twisting trails through the tawny hills; to the sandwich and to the pipe, so tasteful, in the mellow noontime sun by the orchard wall. That part of it is just fine. But once your gauntlet is down, once you have started the prowl, you either haul yourself into one piece, or you go home with nothing but a branch of bittersweet and aching

[119]

bunions.

We cite as an instance of proper partridge tactics none other than the President of the Old Duck Hunters' Association, Inc., who has long sensed the rural delights of this bird and its season, but who never, on the quest, lets up an instant. We think we know how his mind works on them, for he is our teacher.

Once a bird is grassed, once Mister President has leveled fair and square, he allows himself a moment's relaxation. He just turns off the steam definitely; so if another bird gets up, he is prepared for being taken unawares. That is, he does nothing by pre-arranged agreement with his own immortal self. He has a little ceremony to perform then.

He picks up the bird. First he studies it to see if it is copper-hued or gray-hued. If it is the latter, he spreads out the miraculous fan and says: "Hmm-m-m. Seeing more of these every year, it seems. Understand they're more common in Canada. Sort of like the brown ones, though, but I don't know...."

Then he straightens out the mussed feathers and strokes the muscled back and hefts the bird with little up-and-down fisherman's hefts. And sure as sin, if the bird is sizable, he'll affirm: "Bet he goes a pound and a half, maybe better."

There is a reverence and a deep appreciation in such scenes as Mister President with a partridge. They tell of Indians and Eskimos going through similar tribal ceremonies at the taking of good trophies. So always we think of Mister President and his first partridge of the hunt, offering to this worthy bird his own accolade and prayer, and that is the way things ought to be.

But soon he comes alive. He cleans the bird then and there, being careful not to remove the vainglorious tail, and he stuffs stiff grass into the cavity, maybe removing one central tail feather for his hat. He wipes his hands on grass, lights his crooked little pipe and sets forth again, a man with a gun on the hunt, hungry like his ancestors and fair, as his kind only can be.

If ever there was an outdoor game that required constant alertness, it is partridge hunting. In a duck blind there are conversational moments. There a man can sweep the horizon and then fill a pipe before taking another look. The same is true of deer hunting. Waiting on a stump in the cut-over, a man can let down a bit — even study the birds that flit near his stand.

But in partridge hunting there is no let-down. You plow through brush, and unless your eyes and ears are on the all-out qui vive a phantom fantail will roar out of thorny cover and leave you standing there like the man who missed the last train home. There must be days for the true partridge hunter when he declares brief armistices, resolved not to raise a stock to shoulder until the pipe has been smoked or the water drunk from the cooling stream. It's that intense.

Some advise that partridge walker-uppers hunt along fairly close together. We are against it. The game is too much touch-and-go. The consciousness of another hunter nearby will slow the fast swing and the sudden adjustment to the roaring throttle of America's noisiest-rising game bird. We believe partridge cronies should keep apart; and if this be a blow at hunting's fraternalism, let the partings call for occasional meetings — in the choke-cherry thicket, by the river bridge, or back at camp, for that matter.

Certainly we like to hunt 'em alone. It helps out that concentration business no end. The brush, the uncertain underfooting, the unnerving get-away are all distraction enough. We'll spin our yarns and trade tobacco with the brethren in between the study periods, when every nerve and muscle must be on the ready.

That lay ahead when the time came to turn the car north and west and poke its nose down the twisty sand trail to a certain cabin by a lake. There was a light in the window at dusk. Mister President, in the old gray sweater vest, waited on the stoop. He was in an unsettled mood.

"There's been a guy around here shooting partridges!" he stormed. "Imagine! Shooting up coveys that have hung around the place all summer. There shouldn't be any bag limit on those kind!"

Which explains a little of Mister President's partridge philosophy. Next to a pot-shooter who busts 'em on the ground, he despises the kind who hunt the lake-cabin precincts, picking up birds that have learned a fatal friendliness for man. When you hunt partridge with Mister President, you get back in there in the bush where the wild, wise brethren scuff in the leaves and success is measured by the soundness of your legs.

In the morning, following the good old habit, we shook shells out of the hunting jacket, put on the thorn-proof duds and announced ourself ready.

Doubtless two less picturesque partridge hunters could be found anywhere. His Honor wore a pair of faded, patched khaki trousers, with light canvas leggings reinforcing his shins. On his feet he wore light boots. His shirt, dug out of some dim closet in the cabin, was a thing minus several buttons and with patches at the elbows.

This was the get-up for partridge for Mister President — and behind him, and me, hung an assortment of fine hunting rags, in great and endless number. But not for partridge. For partridge he has taught me to go in light gear. If it were not for the brambles, he would likely take after them in tennis shoes and shorts.

The night had been cool, with a light frost. The air was still, and even in the early morning there was a haze, promising more haze and warmth. Deer prints from the night's rovings glistened in the frosted sand along the back road from the cabin. The area, in southern Bayfield County, was being visited by a wave of migrating juncos. Half of the year's leaves were gone, promising both profit and loss — easier shooting through the opening woods and noisier footing below, for it was very dry.

"They'll by shy as get-out," forecast Mister President. "Better not talk too much, and walk as quietly as possible. If we just had a good dog —"

He always wishes for a good dog, but admits he never saw one — not on partridge. Oh, he's seen dogs, but not "real partridge dogs."

We walked almost two miles. Over the sandy back road, down across the thoroughfare bridge, then across country, through popple trees and underbrush. Birds were not located. We each ate an apple to quench thirst. The President leaned his back against a hemlock. I could see he was fixing to say "I'll be darned if I know where they are" when a partridge rocketed to safety from beyond the hemlock.

Mister President philosophized: "Darn him! Didn't he know I had my fingers crossed?"

After that our campaign was just automatic. We skirted the hemlock patch, at a good distance apart. Partridge don't fly far at a crack. Not nearly as far as prairie chickens or pheasants.

This bird fell to Mister President, and he smoothed the feathers and extolled the species. We moved along. No more birds.

"Tell you what," he said finally. "Down beyond the end of the lake there's a series of hills. It's been chilly these nights. Bet you, the birds are in there; and if so they'll be on the sunny slopes. A box of shells I get the first one!"

We skirted the lake, going far around a boggy stretch, and then were among the hills. The sunny slopes faced the south, of course; so the President stopped and gave counsel. "We've got to get around and come up on 'em. Partridge will fly uphill if they can have their choice, and in that way there's less chance of them flying straight into our faces. We'll get going away shots — if we're lucky."

We were lucky. We made the detour, knowing four or five good little hills could be covered on the return. Half-way up the first hill, scuffing through sweetfern and blown-down popple, I heard Mister President's gun bark twice off to my left. He was a quarter mile away, but I heard his yell in the still air: "Wanna bet it ain't a double?"

"No more bets!" I shouted back.

Later we met, and he chided me: "I got just the one, but I bluffed you out, cheapskate!"

Up and down and sometimes along the ridges of those hills we went, with stops now and then for Presidential banter. You would like that place. It is a very special place. The sun at partridge time comes there in long slanting shafts. It daubs the leafless popple with bland yellows and grays. You hardly know, mooching along, where the yellow of the autumn sun leaves off and the gray of the popple bark begins.

You wade ankle-deep in the yellow and russet leaves of the popple and the scrub-oak, and every time you claim a partridge and open his craw and smell the clover therein you wonder where the duece he picked it up. Likely his ruffed royalty gobbled those sweet leaves on some near-by tote road. And if you have wondered, you who hunt the North, where the tote-road clover comes from, consider that lumber-camp horses were fed the best of hay.

Yes, indeed, it is a very special place. We had made enough of a detour to take us far back in the hills, so that we had many a southern slope to work. The bottoms of our boots wore shiny, and the intensity of the hunt was a strain, so that in due time Mister President called a halt in a valley. There had been a wind-storm there years back. Big blown-down popple invited us to sit. Munching sandwiches, we talked. Or rather, I listened.

"Take this partridge here in Wisconsin. He hasn't been bragged up like he ought to be. We've done a swell job putting over the muskie, and the deer, too. But how many people know about this partridge — really know him? And how many treat him as he deserves? Like yesterday, when that fellow was around the lake cabins busting 'em on the ground — A man who'll bust partridge on the ground should be hanged!"

He shrugged his shoulders and dropped the subject. He might have gone on, but there was no need of it. I knew what was in his mind. He is a man with praise for a grand bird. He would, had he chosen, discussed its little-understood comings and goings. He would have said, as he has often: "Some day someone is going to find out what makes these partridge die off, and he is going to cure it, so the crop stays put; and when that happens, you'll see something. Yep, they'll find out the exact relation of the cycle to ticks, cover, habits. They'll do it."

No game-management expert, Mister President nevertheless has a deep and full understanding of the problems besetting the experts. You learn from the President of the Old Duck Hunters that nobody knows it all and that there is room for two kinds of wildlife management — by the technical boys and the men like himself, with only one button on the old duck-hunting mackinaw.

We topped off our lunch with apples. The next hill beckoned. Like the others, it was a jackstraw heap of down stuff, rotting and tangled among the upright trees. We separated, and not long after three birds roared out of my path.

One bore to the right, in a straight plane, thank heaven. I knew he was mine as the right barrel was squeezed off. There was one more in range. Sensing that is pretty instinctive and pretty quick. It's the now-or-never thought that flashes through the partridge hunter's mind. I caught him by swinging left and ahead as he made for dense popple, and when he tumbled I marked the spot by a burned rampike.

He could wait. The rampike was his address. The first I had neglected to mark, for all the trees around him looked alike. However, he was close, and I was lucky; and when I picked him up there in the leaves, I knew I'd find the other. I did, and my shout rang out among the hills.

Mister President worked over toward me and examined them.

"That one there," he said, "is a cock. His ruff pattern is carried out right across his breast, and he's big. That other one may be a hen. The ruff is smaller. It don't come 'round in front like a cock's. Still I wouldn't bet on that second bird, although I'm positive that other one is a rooster. We'll be quitting now."

"Quitting! And two more to go — apiece? We can get 'em — you and I - in the next mile."

The President of the Old Duck Hunters grinned, a bit wearily, for he is much older than I and the going had been hard. There was a note of tenderness in his voice, and there, in a flash, was the story of partridge, straight from one who loves them best and hunts them hard.

[124]

"Sure. Sure, we can get 'em. But we've got a brace apiece."
A brace apiece. Who shall ask for more?

I think this is the best story ever written about the outdoors. I remember well the impact it had on me when I read it first in 1944. It is, of course, another of the great MacQuarrie statements — the curative effect of the outdoors on a person.

It's also a mighty theme to bring to life within the shallow confines of an all too short, short story. It is MacQuarrie's mastery at its best. There are four parts: The stage is set, so briefly but so well. Then the author intensifies the characterization by emphasizing the hardship of the outdoors. Then with infinite sublety coming at you as smoothly as a perfectly thrown slider, MacQuarrie changes from the man going down to the man starting back up. After you read it for enjoyment, go back and see where and how he does it. Finally, there is the brief but perfect close. "That's him all right."

That MacQuarrie keeps it tightly within the bounds of credibility — one false note would shatter it — it is a marvel. There's nothing I know of in outdoor literature to match it.

Nervous Breakdown

For one thing, there was that confoundedly efficient Miss Benson. Always at him, she was. "Good morning, Mr. Jones....Mr. Smith to see you, Mr. Jones....Will you sign these, Mr. Jones?...Goodnight, Mr. Jones."

What was he thinking of, anyway? Gertrude Benson was the finest secretary in New York. Snap out of it, Bill Jones. You're certainly going balmy in the head!

He dropped the fishing-camp folder in the waste basket and turned to his desk. Too old, he thought. Should have done it twenty years ago. But twenty years ago the kids were hardly more than babies, and there was Mom and a job.

Now that the kids were grown, Mom was coddling him more than ever. Yes, coddling him! Dear Mom, always thinking of someone other than herself. Mom could see no sense in a browse bed — "Will! At your age, sleeping on the ground!"

He picked up the memorandum which Miss Benson had left. Mr. Blake of National Metals at 9:30; Mr. Peddy of Empire Sales at 10; senior committee meeting at 11:00. His gaze strayed to the waste basket. The folder said: "Off the beaten track...the last frontier...our guides really take you back in there..."

Fifty-five years old, with a belly and a half million dollars. He looked out the window, off across the tops of the tall buildings. Thirty-five years of it, from clerk to a vice-presidency. Mom and the kids were very proud of him. They thought it screamingly funny when he took off a week or two and went fishing.

A pigeon, city vagabond of the species, yet somehow wild and free among skyscraper chasms, landed on the window sill. Miss Benson, who forgot nothing, had spread the daily ration of grain. The bird pecked. His thoughts dreamed away. . . .

He could tell Mom he was taking a guide so that she would not worry. There was country up there, country for a man to see. Not with a guide — not this time. This was something he had to do for himself. Last summer Hanson, the guide on the fringes of this country, had told him it was solid wilderness north to the Arctic Circle. He remembered Hansons' grin as he explained: "During the depression, when guiding fell off, I spent a season up in there. Got lost a-purpose. Never had such a good time in my life!"

No, he would not be afraid. He had not been afraid as a boy in Pennsylvania when he had camped out on his own trap-line. He might break a leg. Sure! He might get bumped by a truck in town, too.

Miss Benson found him staring out the window. Brisk, efficient Miss Benson, whose words were as crisp as her tailored clothes. He hated Miss Benson. He wanted to say, "Damn it, Gerty, why don't you leave me alone?"

"Mr. Jones of National Metals to see you, sir."

He wanted to answer, "Tell him to go to the devil." He must have telegraphed the thought to Miss Benson, for she frowned. "I'm tired, Miss Benson," he said. "Mr. Pitcairn knows about this order. I suggest—"

"Yes, sir. I'll see Mr. Pitcairn right away. I hope everything is all right." There was real anxiety in her voice.

He smiled at her and suddenly did not hate her at all. It was ridiculous to hate Miss Benson. A brick, she was. Good as a man — yes, better than a man.

"Am I cracking up?" he wondered. It was something he could not quite put his finger on. He wasn't interested in his work the way he had been. The consuming passion to try the impossible was gone. For months he had found himself making an effort to do things. It wasn't like him. Was that why Mom hovered around him? She did hover!

His phone tinkled distantly in the big room. It was Banks, the president. Good old Banks — solid, sensible, old Banks.

"Miss Benson mentioned you weren't feeling well. I don't want to intrude. I'm rather awkward about such things. I'm wondering—"

"Mr. Banks, I have got to get out of here." His own words surprised him. He hadn't meant to say it quite that way.

"I'll be right in," Banks said.

He came, cool and steady as always. He came smiling and walked across the heavy rug. "Fellow," he said, "you don't look good to me." It was like Banks to speak his mind.

"Banks—" He could go no further. He was choked up.

Banks put a firm hand on his shoulder. "Spit it out. We've always worked that way."

For five minutes he talked. He talked rapidly, and at times his eyes shone. When he had finished, Banks laughed.

"Fine!" he said. "I'd rather you'd take a guide, but do it your way. I respect your way, as I always have."

He fidgeted. "Banks, is this a nervous breakdown?"

"Some call it that."

"Mom will want to get a doctor."

"I think you've written your own prescription."

"I—"

"Nuts!" said J. Forsythe Banks, leader of industry. "Don't let me see you around here in the next month. Git!"

Mom had been difficult, he thought as the train carried him north out of Duluth. But she had felt better about it when he lied cheerfully and said he was taking a cook as well as a guide.

The conductor came through and eyed him. "Lookin' up timber?"

"Yes. Be sure and wake me at six. I want to see the country."

His eyes were open long before the porter came to jerk at the green curtain of his berth. In the September dawn there flashed by an endless land of prim stunted spruce, pink-gray boulders and lakes that seemed to be waiting for someone to come and use them. He put away the business suit and climbed into store new wool. He had to rip the price tag off the checked flannel shirt.

He transferred personal items to the rough clothing that felt so good, then folded his pin-striped doublebreasted suit and handed it to the porter to be shipped back to the hotel in Duluth.

"Yes suh, 'deed, suh. We is about two hours from Nine Mile water-tank."

He ate a huge breakfast, for he would not want to stop at noon to boil the kettle.

[129]

At the water-tank, where the train stopped, he hurried forward to the baggage car and helped with the unloading of the canoe and gear. The train pulled out. His dunnage beside the water-tank made a formidable pile. A hundred yards away lay the edge of Wabigoon Lake. Long before he had toted all the stuff to the rocky lake shore he was weary. He fastened the tiny motor to the bracket of the 15-foot canoe and set forth. The outfitter in town had insisted on the small canoe. "It's a 60-pounder. A two-man job would break your back on the portages."

He had to stop and trim the load so that the bow dropped. After that his speed increased. From an aluminum fishing rod tube he took out a roll-up map of Ontario. Wabigoon looked pretty big the way he was going, north.

He felt free, yet he was anxious. Could he do all the things as well as Hanson had done them? He went over the outfit item by item. The fellow in the store knew his business. He had told this clerk that he had wanted to go with canoe and paddle. The man had insisted on the tiny motor and ten gallons of fuel.

"If you run out of fuel and have to come home light, throw away everything you don't need, including the motor," he had said.

Yes, the outfitter knew his business. He was traveling six miles an hour in a light chop. Almost 160 pounds of equipment, fuel and man in a craft that weighed 60 pounds. By noon the wind had picked up, but a boyhood sense for water had returned. He caught the knack of running on the lee side of the islands. In the open reaches he learned to jockey the waves by quartering into them and away from them.

In the late afternoon, more than forty miles from the put-in, he chose a spruce-grown island for the night. It had a wind-swept point where the late-season mosquitoes would not be present. The island looked like some ancient sea-faring craft, with spruce trees for masts and sails. He cut the motor and swung in. Just before the nose of the canoe touched land the sharp edge of a rock slashed a six-inch gash in the canvas. He would have to be more careful in landing hereafter.

It took an hour to build a fire, heat the tiny can of marine glue, and "iron on" a canvas patch with heated rocks. He scorched a finger doing it. A blister ballooned up.

He longed for a deep, soft chair to sink into, like one at the club or his easy chair at home. And a highball and the evening paper. And an evening meal on a white tablecloth. He unpacked gear and dived into the woods with an ax for browse.

It was near dark when the silk tent was pitched and the air mattress spread over the browse. The wind went down, and his breezy point attracted its quota of mosquitoes. The sunset was tremendous behind spires of spruce. But he did not enjoy it. He lay down awhile before starting to prepare supper. It had been like that for a long time. He wanted to lie down and look at a job before beginning it. In other days he had just pitched in.

He was hungry. How did guides like Hanson manage things so deftly on the ground? He struggled with the fire, which got too hot and then too cold. He burned his other hand. The loons of Wabigoon struck up their song, and he became definitely lonely and uncertain of himself. Just how smart was he in going away by himself without a guide.

By trial and error he adjusted the reflector baker so that the biscuits got done, though some were doughy and some burned. The dried soup which he spilled into the stew-pan swelled enormously and overflowed into the fire. The tea was more like tannin, steeped too long. He must remember to do that last.

The supper did not taste good. The soup got cold and the tea stayed hot. Washing dishes was a chore. There was no sand on the rocky island with which to scour the dishes. He noted as he washed in the lake that his hands were already creviced with dirt.

Well, he would sleep, anyway. He drew tight the mosquito netting in the tent door and flopped down. He did not sleep. Three mosquitoes had to be hunted down. The browse under his hip was too high and had to be readjusted. When this was done, he was nervously wide awake. He tossed in the sleeping bag. It was after midnight when he dozed off.

A few hours later the flapping of the tent awakened him. The wind was shaking it. There was a bright glow through the green tent. He leaped up. The wind had fanned the embers of his cooking fire, and sparks were flying. Without pausing to put on boots, he grabbed a folding bucket and dashed to the lake. He stubbed his toe and swore. it took a half dozen pailfuls to extinguish the fire, and by then the wind had torn out the stakes on one side of the tent.

In the dark he replaced the stakes, as deep as he could in the thin soil, and anchored them with rocks. He tightened the ridge rope by lifting the shear poles front and back. The rain caught him as he finished. It came horizontally from the west, cold and stabbing — a fall rain. Inside the tent, he lit the aluminum lantern's single fat candle and lay on his back. He fell asleep from sheer exhaustion.

In the morning he felt as though he had not slept at all. The long water hop of the previous day had brought the reflected sun up beneath his hat brim. His face was painfully burned. The oatmeal he cooked was good, but the taste of powdered milk on it was unfamiliar. Mom, right now, was in the breakfast nook, having the kind of breakfast he wanted. If he were there, she would wheel the car up and honk and he would get in and they would drive away and the traffic cops would wave cheerfully.

As it was, he faced a run with the canoe and then a two-mile portage. He dreaded it. If only Hanson were here to take over!

The portage was worse than he had anticipated. It had been a wet September. There was one low spot of a hundred yards where he waded to his knees, feeling the trail with his boots. The gear was in two packsacks. Then there was the canoe, the motor and the two tins of fuel, each weighing thirty pounds.

As long as he lived he would not forget that portage! Hanson had said that this portage was what kept a lot of trippers from going back in there. Even the good guides did not like it. The sweat ran into his eyes. He drank quarts of water at either end of the punishing trail. Pack straps cut his shoulders. He could not complete the job in the day. He left the canoe and motor until next day and hurried camp in the rain. Just in time, too. A needle-fine rain of the lasting kind came down. He gulped hot soup and eased himself into the sleeping bag.

He slept. He slept like a log. In the morning, still groggy, he put on a rain jacket and limped back for the canoe and motor.

The lake before him had no name on the map. It was just a number put there by a surveyor, Lake One. There were others, named and numbered, stretching beyond to the north. He rigged a casting rod and took a four-pound wall-eyed pike with the third cast. He was using a pork-rind lure, but he felt he might have done as well with a clothes-pin bearing hooks.

In the rain he dressed the fish and baked it in the reflector oven with rashers of bacon. He brewed his coffee carefully and saw to it that the biscuits browned evenly. It all tasted good. He ate it, watching a moose on the far shore of the lake. When he had finished, a Canada jay came to his plate and dined. The bird was unafraid and greedy.

The skies cleared in the early afternoon, and he set off. He portaged out of Lake One to another, Lake Three on the map. The portage was a mere

hundred-yard haul-over, up a hogback, down the other side. Without waiting to set up camp he cast the pork rind from the shore. A 10-pound northern took it. He got in the canoe and fished the shore. The water was alive with northern pike and wall-eyed pike. It was a carnival of fishing. He saved one for supper.

There was a white frost in the night. He felt it coming before bedtime so he folded back the canoe tent to make a lean-to and built a roaring fire before it. By the firelight he ate, picking the firm pike flesh from his plate with his fingers and wondering what Mom would say if she could have seen him. Owls were abroad, and beaver were working not far away. He tidied up camp and lay in the sleeping bag. The last thing he remembered was the strong whistle of wings. Ducks on the move...He fell asleep.

For a week he stayed at this place. Mornings he killed a duck or two, reaching for them with a .410 as they came low across a pass. There were mornings when he might have killed a hundred. All he wanted was enough to eat. Each morning it seemed colder and the white frost heavier. The birch leaves had been yellowish when he began the trip. Now there were gone. The wild-cherry leaves were brown and drying. Sumac groves were carmine. The song birds were gone except for an occasional flicker. He was busy, and the days passed quicker than he cared to see them pass.

It was while he walked around this lake to retrive a wave-borne mallard that he realized he was not tired! It was a long walk of three miles to where the wind and waves carried the mallard. He thought it would be better for him to walk it than to take the canoe. He picked up the bird.

Ten days of wilderness had made his trousers gape at the waist. One day he permitted himself the luxury of a shave. To his surprise, his face was not left raw and razor-chopped. The skin had toughened. It had had a chance to heal itself from incessant, hurried scrapings.

His appetite amazed him. He found he was no longer dragging himself to camp tasks. He went at them eagerly and did them efficiently. There was always something to do — too much, in fact. The days were too short. They zipped by. He broke out his camera and renewed an old hobby. He built a table and chair for the camp. He fed the trusting whisky-jacks and stalked the shore-line moose, and counted it a red-letter day when he got close enough to one to touch it with a paddle. He was no longer lonely. There was life and activity all about him.

He pushed north from this camp for a steady week, through many lakes, over endless portages. Almost every night the aurora borealis spread over the heavens. Every morning his boots were stiff with frost. A porcupine gnawed his sweat-saturated paddle, and he spent half a day chopping down a spruce and fashioning another with ax and knife. He was inordinately proud of that paddle. Just as he was proud of the neat patching he put on the tent where camp-fire sparks burned through its walls.

The routine of making camp was so perfected that he could slide the canoe ashore, set up camp, and be eating a meal in a half hour. He found out that the way to eat bacon and fish in a one-man camp was right out of the frying-pan. It saved doing dishes.

He planned and prepared delicious meals and ate them ravenously. Planked fish, bean-hole beans, hot corn-meal muffins. One day he triumphed with his last can of peaches dedicated to a shortcake. In town it would have been enough for four. He licked up the last crumbs and wished he had another can of sliced peaches.

Thin ice in the portage-trail hollow sent him south. He studied the map and penciled out a great arc of travel that would fetch him back by another route. The Nine Mile water-tower was his goal. He was not sure of the date. He had either lost a day or gained a day somewhere. It didn't matter.

It was on a lake named Papoose that he lost the motor. He had neglected to make fast the safety rope to the bracket, and the thrifty egg-beater went down. A weighted fish line showed seventy feet of water, so he did not bother to drag for it. Many miles of paddling and portaging lay before him. He grinned. This is what he had come for: to see how much of him was left. He grinned with anticipation.

First he unscrewed the outboard bracket, threw it away, and heaved overboard the remaining four gallons of fuel. Then he paddled ashore and went over his outfit carefully. Every item was scanned for weight and utility. When he had finished, everything went into one packsack. On the next portage he went across in one trip with canoe and pack.

For five days he paddled and portaged, eating twice a day, morning and evening. It was hard work, but it was good work. His hands had hardened and his back had stiffened before the loss of the motor. They became harder and stiffer. His palms were calloused. In the evenings when he went ashore he welcomed the wilderness with a weary zest. Every place seemed like home, for he was self-sufficient. He got lost for a day and a half by missing a portage trail, but took a short cut back to the penciled route via a new and shorter portage. He wondered what Mom would say when she found him so lean.

"Will! At your age sleeping on the ground!" He laughed. He knew what he would do when he saw Mom. He would sweep her off the floor, and she would protest. "Will, you fool! Let me down!" It had been fifteen years since he had picked up Mom like that. If Mom grew anxious and tried to hover over him again, he would have to spank her, even if one of her grandchildren was present.

On a long, narrow water which the map said was Burnt-over Lake he started supper one night. A seaplane circled, spotted his tent and landed. It taxied in, and the pilot came ashore. He was a commercial flyer, looking for a lost camper. He explained the man's name was William Jones, and that Jones was two days overdue at Nine Mile water-tank. Railway officials had reported that he had not appeared.

"You can stop looking. How bout supper?"

"But you're not lost," said the flyer, who had studied the shipshape camp and the hard brown man.

"Nope, just tardy. Lost my outboard, and I'm paddling in."

"I'll fly you in tonight in a half hour."

"That's what you think."

"A Mr. Banks has asked us to find you."

"Good old Banks."

The flyer sat down to a meal of fresh caught wall-eyed pike, baking-powder biscuits with maple syrup, and hot green tea. He was a nice chap. He took off while there was still a little daylight. In forty-five minutes he was on the phone.

"But are you sure he is all right?" Banks demanded.

"I've lived in this country most of my life. If I needed a guide, I'd hire that bird."

"Does he feel all right?"

"Well, he carried a fifty-pound down log to the fire with one hand."

"Did he say when he would reach Nine Mile?"

"Yes, sir. He said he would get there when he was damn good and ready."

There was a pause and a sigh at the other end of the line. Then Banks said, "That's him, all right."

*After MacQuarrie's death his widow, herself a
writer, and his daughter tried without success to
interest a publisher in putting his stories in book
form. The title they chose was this one:* We Shall
Gather By The Ice House.

*It is a marvelous title with its promise of soft
sweetness. A promise, incidently, more than
delivered in the yarn itself. Seldom has the
author written so emotionally of the country
and type of life he loved.*

*But it isn't a good title for a book. In the first
place, by itself it has no meaning. In contrast, The
Old Duck Hunter's Association, Inc. has. Add to
that (because they aren't all duck stories) the new
Mr. President's description of his writing "been
reading your drivel for years." The "drivel" not
only adds a little bite, more importantly in a word
it instantly characterizes the writer for the modest,
self-effacing man he was.*

We Shall
Gather By The Icehouse

There are corners of this green footstool which men look upon with more than mere gratefulness — places where they feel deeply at home. Let all of them choose their own inviolate acres. Along the banks of the raging Rogue, or in the pine-clad hills of Alabama. All of the close-to-earth hunting and fishing men know their chosen places.

My chosen corner is scrubby enough. Even the President of the Old Duck Hunters has joked: "I doubt if the Indians would take it back if we offered it to 'em," but his talk fools nobody. For the chosen corner, a man is always ready to fight.

One day Mister President suggested that we cease exploring the far partridge cover of North Wisconsin and get back to first principles. He suggested that we shove off in the briar-proof pants and the far-going boots for "the best derned partridge country in Wisconsin, which starts right at your doorstep on the Middle Eau Claire Lake." He referred, of course, to *Banasa umbellus*, the fantailed power-house known all through upper Wisconsin as plain old "paterdge."

"All right," I said, for I have always retained a formal vote in affairs of the Old Duck Hunters' Association, even though his word is law.

That was in the "early bird season" we have here in Wisconsin, not to be confused with the "late season," when leaves are gone and birds are sought in frostier weather. But we never did get together in that early season. Other things intervened.

We met in late October, when the scrub was afire with purples and reds, in the manner that scarlet oak preserves its glory long after color has fled from less tenacious trees. We met at my shack on the middle lake at sun-up. It had been a long drive for me — some three hours of hunching over the wheel, figuring out a nasty ground fog. The President, who tolerates and even loves me, after his kind, and who was waiting there for me when the sun rolled up over the Norways across the lake, said that I looked like a saucer of cool coffee with too much cream in it.

He also said that it was a caution the way folks nowadays tear hell-bent around the country at all hours — and would I come into the house and consume (a) three scrambled eggs, (b) eight rashers of home-smoked bacon, (c) four cups of coffee, and (d) "a hatful of oven-hard toast?"

I would. He sat there and laughed at me, puffing on his crooked pipe. He has always laughed at me. I am flattered by it. Mostly when he is laughing at me he is scheming up some way to teach me about partridge or mallards, or of mice and men, or how to hang a deer without breaking my back.

One of the nice things about owning my own shack in that country is that I am always a guest when the President is on hand. The place is just like the country around it. Everything fits in like old boots and wool socks.

I got up from his repast and seized dishes. But he stopped that instantly.

"How many times must I tell you never to be caught washing dishes in October early in the morning?"

A complex man, you might say. On the other hand, you might say he is merely a man with common sense. At any rate, the dishes were abandoned over my objections, which drew from him the suggestion that if I was so damn neat I could stay home and darn some socks for him.

There we were, on that sparkly morning, surveying from the stoop of the shack a world of such benign goodness that even the red squirrels wouldn't cuss it. We stood there on the stoop, each in his briar-proof pants, each with a shotgun under the arm. Hizzoner looked up the glory of sunlight on frosted pines and recalled: "Only fellow I ever wanted to hang worked in my garage. One morning I heard him say, 'Take a look out the window. That damn sun is shining again!' I fired him."

Then he added: "I've got this all planned. You take the thoroughfare country, and I'll work south and west below you and meet you by the old ice-house on Libby Bay at sunset."

I protested. He was giving me the best country. He was also giving himself a terrific walk and possibly a wading with gun, boots and pants held aloft, across the river-like thoroughfare which connects two lakes.

"Do as I say," he directed. "You'll see some birds and some ducks, too. I've had my fling down there. In case I'm ahead of you, I'll leave a note tucked into one of the logs on the ice-house."

Then he left me. No use to protest further. He took a firmer grip on his shotgun and strode up the sandy, rising road.

To the south lay an undulating country grown to scrub-oak and jack-pine, with low spots of spruce and tamarack and here and there some isolated stands of magnificent Norways. My job, as directed, was to push through the scrub cover and explore vagrant hardwood patches for ruffed grouse. Then I was to cross the thoroughfare bridge and explore the very rugged hills lying east and south of the thoroughfare before they fell off gradually to the lake.

A fetching prospect. I realized that — after I was on the way over country so crisscrossed with deer trails that whenever one was lost another going the same direction could be found in a few seconds. I realized, too, that Mister President had been more than generous. But then that is his way. It takes such a philosopher as the President of the Old Duck Hunters to perceive that a man should renew acquaintanceship, on his own, with beloved country.

Only when a fellow is very young or when he is greatly uplifted does he experience the spiritual exaltation of such glorious morning expeditions. Such bright, solitary rambles in the morning remind one of long-gone days when the circus came to town and a fellow got up, shivering in the dawn, to hit the canvas boss for a job.

The shaded earth under the trees was frosty damask. In the jack-pine tops the sun varnished a billion needles. It was easy to find the way. I had been there many times — in all seasons.

Ahead of me, in that dip, I'd worked my first hunting dog. Beyond, in still lower ground, I'd made a double on partridge. Farther on was a place where I'd missed a standing buck....

In the first big Norway grove four partridges dynamited out of the sunny, open ground beneath the round ruddy boles. They made it safely to dense cover. I thought, ejecting the two shells, it was a good thing Mister President was not around to see that sort of performance.

The grove did not let me down entirely. The four fast birds had thrown me into gear so that when a single roared out thirty yards beyond I cut him down just in time. Hunting men know the feeling! On your own, with your own worn shotgun. Best of all — in your own country, the kind of country so familiar that you feel like tipping your hat to old landmarks. And they say folks won't fight for that?

This was one of those peak partridge years, such as Wisconsin has had for three seasons. These are years of huge coveys, when bag limits are easy.

I wondered how Mister President was getting along. I wondered if he were completely happy without me there to be bossed. I wondered if his aging legs were taking it all right, and laughed aloud then, for I have yet to see the cover which his whipcord thighs cannot bust.

After the Norway grove there was the edge of the thoroughfare. This is a good hunting space of about a half mile. Paper birches and young Norway pines contest to see which shall win. In this place the well-worn deer trails are closer together than ever.

So help me, there was a partridge in a cherry tree. It sat as I approached, and I waited for it to steam out. It did, too. It steamed right over my head so close that I feared to fire. My only alibi is that I didn't have a chance. I didn't even let go with the speculative right barrel as it darted through the branches.

I worked that half-mile patch dutifully, I went south by the thoroughfare, negotiating the lumpy hills and the whippy brush; but I encountered only birds flushing wild, fifty yards ahead, which is as good as a thousand yards away in that cover.

Back along the thoroughfare I went to the little hump-backed bridge. There I stopped to look down into six feet of clear water where some good smallmouths were still occupying the bridge hole. One sunny afternoon in this hole, with a yellow feather minnow — But enough of that. This is hunting.

I crossed the bridge and studied the winding sand trail before me, trying to keep my eyes at their best wide-angle aperture so as to be ready for roadside birds. I seldom fail here.

Two partridge blasted out of a wet spot where I have been wont to dig angle-worms in summer. While I shot I wondered if they like worms, just a woodcock do. After picking up my bird I looked at the damp spaded ground. No earth-worms were in sight.

[142]

After that there were more hills, heavily grown — hills of popple, both standing and down stuff. Hills with thick growths of young Norways. Hills as bare as your hand, except for sedge grasses.

It was in one of these sloping, sedgy places that a veritable multitude of sharptails leaped out. Being in a quick-reflex partridge-hunting mood, I caught one as he set his wings to float into distant cover. Sure, I should have doubled. But his fluffy speckled highness contrasted well with the partridge already suspended at my belt by a cord.

Now I was on the opposite side of the thoroughfare. The autumn morning was building itself into a symphony. The President had mentioned something about ducks in the thoroughfare.

So for perhaps a half hour I Indian-hunted the thoroughfare edge, taking advantage of high grass and clumps of popple and birch. My mind was completely off upland birds when a single partridge roared out from my left and was gone in a flash.

I kicked myself for not being ready. But it is always so. One thing at a time, they do say, is the way for a hunter to hunt. I think that if I had been hunting partridge I'd have nailed that fellow. But my mind was on what might materialize from the thoroughfare — in close, where succulent grasses could be reached by tip-up ducks.

Near the end of my river-bank beat, at a place where I used to bet nickels with Mister President as to which side of a log a snapping turtle would jump off, I heard a faint gabble. It was indeed faint, but not far off. The grass smothered the sound. I worked toward it. The sound grew.

One gabby hen mallard was simply telling everything to the whole neighborhood. When I got quite close, I could hear the cautious "mee-amph" of a drake. Maybe he was chiding her for her garrulity. He should have borne down harder, considering what happened.

Through the grass I made out three mallards, all in range. I exchanged the 7½'s, new crimps, for chilled 6's. Then I waited, enjoying the spectacle reserved for the sneak hunter who gets close enough to study them without being detected.

The three increased to five. The five increased to nine. By that time I was thinking that when they jumped it would be a good idea to pick a crossing shot with the first barrel.

Perhaps I could have stalked within ten yards of them, but the tension was growing. At twenty-five yards I stood up. The hen quit gabbling. There was that still-as-death pause which comes when the gauntlet is

[143]

down.

They bounded out, and the crossing shot clicked perfectly for a hen and a drake. But so quickly were they making way that the choke barrel had to reach for the third bird, another drake. He slanted in his fall and provided me with a 75-yard wading job in water not half as warm as the Indian-summer air.

Drying blue-cold legs, I had a moment to gloat upon the bag. Meager enough, but a great and varied treasure there in the sunny brown grass by the thoroughfare. A treasure from my very own country.

Isn't that the whole box score in a nutshell? Isn't it simply that all of us like to go once in a while to our own home acres and collect with judicious rod and careful gun the respective crops as they accumulate with the seasons?

East of the thoroughfare, beyond tangled northern woods and rough hills jack-strawed with timber, there spread a stretch of blue water. It is the upper end of the lake, or Libby Bay. Naturally, I thought more of it after the encounter with the mallards.

I hit the cover on the way to the lake and picked off another partridge. Once I bragged to a fellow that in one season I never missed a partridge on the wing. Not having grown up with these birds, he was distinctly skeptical. He still is, and I don't blame him. What I meant was that I never missed one that I was ready for!

This third bird was, I suppose, a cock. Anyway, he was big, the feather pattern on his breast went all the way across, and he wore a continuous dark band across his tail. Let 'em argue if they choose; I think he was a cock.

The lake burst upon me as I topped a hill strewn with downed popple. These were victims of erratic tornadic winds which sometimes float off their northward course, going up the Mississippi, and find their way along the feeder streams to the big creek, striking here and there.

From the hilltop I saw the stretch of lake known as Libby Bay. There, riding the little waves and soaking in the sun, were significant black dots. Bluebills, of course! Fattest, swiftest, huskiest ducks for their inches that fly upon the face of the North American continent.

I skirted the clean, sandy edge of the lake and occupied a blunt point of land where Libby Bay had its largest indentation of the shore-line. Ducks were not moving to any extent. Only now and then would a restless single break away. I sprawled in soft sand beneath jack-pines crowding the lake edge. It was warm. Spiders labored inches from my nose.

I settled the shotgun in the jack-pine branches and lay back, hands under head. I drowsed, like the ducks. Maybe a couple could fly over. Maybe....

Now, as I write it, I cannot tell what awakened me. It may have been the sand, which cools quickly under a man in October. But then it may have been the knifing whistle of short, swift wings overhead. Anyway, before I could manage to come alive, a flock of about twenty bluebills was over me and gone.

But there were new sounds in the upper air to soothe my sense of defeat. New and magic sounds, growing stronger. No need to tell how it is. The bald facts are that another flock was busting across my blunt-nosed point with a confidence learned from weeks of doing the same thing without endangering themselves. The point is a short cut from mid-Libby Bay and its wild celery to the lower thoroughfare and another lake where more celery grows.

Here was a situation calling for calculation. No dog to retrieve downed birds in deep water; no boat within two miles. I waited until the birds were well over the point. Two of them hit the sandy ground with that lead-weighted thump which all bluebill shooters know.

Well..Partridge. A "chicken." Mallards — two drakes! A couple of those ocean-going tugs known as bluebills.

Hizzoner himself would approve such a nicely balanced bag. He would size them up critically and say, "Not too many; just enough."

It was time for me to push back along the lake shore to the ice-house rendezvous. No more hunting now. Just going home. Just the familiar old dilapidated ice-house, with Mister President waiting there to take the wind out of my sails.

No more tense muscles. Let the partridge leap out if they wished. They were safe. This was the armistice at the end of the day which is declared by hunting men in favor of their dearest enemies.

Walking along with the weight at my belt, I remembered what Mister President had said about home. "I dunno...I always like to go away, and I always like to come back."

The sun got well down. Purple built up in the east. I saw a grand buck. I hit the clearing by the old ice-house, hoping Mister President would be there. He'd be company for the mile hike homeward.

He was not there. But he had been there. His tracks were unmistakable in the soft sand before the ice-house door. His message was written on a shell-box tucked in a log crack: "I'm going on ahead to start the coffee." That was all.

Today muskies are all over the place. The spread of these mean-looking fish is a triumph of fish biology. In MacQuarrie's day they were rigidly localized. But so many people went after them, bringing their dollars as well as their fishing rods, they were called the fish that built the schools in northen Wisconsin.

They are still there, of course. This one, like all of MacQuarrie's stories, is timeless. Everything here could be duplicated tomorrow. There are muskie fanatics that whittle their own plugs and heave them after the big pike. I didn't even edit out the 1928 automobile. I've been seeing a lot of those too lately.

Muskies Lardin' Up

It was so cold that November evening that a neighborhood dog, drifting home for supper, lifted a paw from the frigid cement sidewalks when he paused to sniff out the homeward route. I came through the park and felt the frozen turf underfoot. In the house on the corner, where the President of the Old Duck Hunters' Association, Inc., dwells, a light gleamed from a basement window. Turning in at my own door, I surmised that the Old Man was plucking some late-season ducks.

So after a late supper, I went across the street to help. He was down there among the old trunks, beneath the pipes of the heating system — whittling. He was not cleaning ducks. He was whittling.

"Tomorrow," he announced, "we'll go fishing."

I could hardly believe my ears. And I was disappointed at not getting just one more whack at the tardier migrants. Even late in the duck season it is ritual for the Old Duck Hunters to hunt ducks. This singular corporation has hunted ducks when it was possible to walk out on the ice and place the decoys — being careful to remove the anchor cords!

He showed me his whittling job — a fish bait. It was a foot long, shaped from native white cedar. He said he had planned to make it look like a mud-puppy, but each one turned out more like a sucker; so he guessed it was a sucker.

The floor and the work-bench told the story. He had committed offhand surgery on a 12-inch cedar fence post. Half-whittled mud-puppies and suckers lay among the shavings.

"I'd have got her right the first time if I'd had a spoke-shave," he explained. "Hand me that coffee can."

He snipped pieces of tin from the can and fitted tail, fins and nose-piece to the virgin bait. The wood of the tail was so thin that the brads holding the horizontally affixed tail split the wood, but he just wrapped wire around it and said, "She'll hold." He screwed in treble hooks at strategic places, and fixed a screen door eye screw in the head. He took silver and gold radiator paint and daubed it on, adding a dash of red over that blend.

"That'll get 'em," he said, holding it up for me to admire.

"Whales?"

"Muskies. Lyman Lake muskies."

"There are still some ducks in the country on the rivers and lake thoroughfares."

I hate to give up on ducks, having hunted them in December in north Wisconsin when the temperature has been quite a bit below zero. But he was bound to fish muskies. There is no use in fighting against him when he is in a determined mood, any more than it is worthwhile trying to beat him down on the price of a used automobile.

All of which explains why, next morning, I went across the street in the dark cold with a rod and a tackle box instead of a shotgun and a shell-box. Loading my equipment into his car, I noted he had included his canvas-shrouded shotgun with the duffel; but when I suggested that I go get mine, and possibly a few decoys, he said he didn't want duck hunting to interfere too much with fishing.

"Not today," he said. "I hanker for a fish."

I drove the chosen vehicle, a locomotive-like contraption of the vintage 1928. We went south, choosing the proper county trunk highways. He sat beside me, adjusting the tin accessories on the cedar-bait monstrosity. He held it low so that the single dash-light would illumine it. He adjusted the tin fins this way and that. It had dried fairly well during the night. The wet spots got rubbed dry on the car upholstery — what was left of it.

He did not need to tell me where to go. In an hour's time I had the big crate in the yard of a man named Jerry, an old logger who had grown up with the country. In his younger days Jerry drove the streams. In his latter days he guarded the dam which held the level of Lyman Lake to its statutory height. He also moulded his own bullets, tapped his own sugar maples, and kept a boat or two handy on the beach for a select few. I digress to tell more about Jerry.

He learned from the Indians how to tan buckskin by the deer-brains and smoke-tan system, actually improving on their methods. He had a way of producing skins of even thickness throughout, and not burned to parchment in some spots, such as often happens when the squaw leaves the hide too long over a smoking fire that gets too hot. The buckskin which he produced was white as chalk and limp as the best chamois.

Conniving gentlemen, like myself, offered him outrageous prices for these rare, medicine-lodge hides. Jerry declined all offers. As long as he could make chopper's mitts out of them and sell them to farmers at 50 cents per pair he was satisfied.

"Gives me something to do in the winter," he explained.

For many years Jerry had been an auxiliary to the Old Duck Hunters. As such, it was only natural to expect that he would have a boat on the shore. We crept by his house so as not to waken him and found our boat. We transferred gear. The Old Man brought forth a sack of duck decoys from the trunk, to my surprise.

"Don't get excited," he warned. "Just brought 'em along with us in case."

We set out on Lyman Lake with the thermometer around 25 above. Mister President took the first turn at the oars, exercising his seniority right to get warmed up. There is no duck-blind cold like fishing-craft cold in the late season. In duck blinds you can at least stamp your feet. Stamp your feet in one of Jerry's boats, and you'll have to frog it to shore!

Lyman Lake is one of three bodies in this farthest north Wisconsin county which contains muskies. The other two are Amnicon Lake and Bear Lake. Lyman and Amnicon are connected by a creek. Both of them drain into Lake Superior via the Amnicon River. In this respect they are similar to the Presque Isle chain in northwestern Vilas County, Wisconsin — Big Crab, Van Vliet, etc. — which drain into Lake Superior via the turbulent Presque Isle River, running north across Michigan's upper peninsula. Most of the Wisconsin muskie waters are tributary to the Chippewa and Flambeau rivers.

Daylight grew, and when we had reached the quaggy south end of Lyman Lake, Mister President's cheeks were ruddy and the old mackinaw was open for ventilation. He turned the oars over to me and occupied the rear seat with his kit. Again he admired the whittled gargoyle. He groped in his long green tackle box for a reel and a bronze wire leader.

[151]

Then he strung up his stiff, five-foot bamboo casting rod, and when I had worked fairly close to shore he said, "Now go slow."

He pounded the edge of floating bog with the home-made plug. A skillful and resourceful man, he made that resurrected cedar fence-post do everything a plug can be made to do by being drawn through water on a 40-pound line. Often he readjusted the tail and tin nose-piece. The coffee-can tin was pretty limp, and had to be bent into shape every third cast or so. He manipulated the bait and maneuvered with the retrieve so that he had that bait coming through the water at various depths and with various wiggles.

I rounded the south bay of the lake, watching the sky for vagrant ducks. He kept on casting, or rather heaving. So large a bait must necessarily be cast out carefully on even so heavy a line as a 40-pounder.

My interest in muskie fishing was less than nil — had been from the start-off. At that moment the Old Duck Hunters might have been keeping house in a tidy point blind on some river thoroughfare where a bluebill came by once in a while. When a dozen mallards leaped up from the shore bog, I wanted to quit fishing, get in there and stick up a blind and see if they would come back for more dabbling.

"Row," said the President of the Old Duck Hunters' Association.

He took off the heavy mackinaw and operated the cedar invention in his worn gray sweater vest. A bundle of bluebills hustled across the lake, and I pointed them out eagerly.

"Row, pup!" he commanded.

We stirred up further ducks, for it was a dark, heavy day. I knew full well the peak of the flight had passed this country, but that is neither here nor there. Every mention I made of sanguinary contact with ducks brought the same reply: "Row!"

How I rowed! I practically circumnavigated Lyman Lake while he fooled with that whittled wonder. I had no faith in it at all. We were back in the neighborhood of Jerry's home on the sugar-maple point so early that Jerry was still abed.

Off the south end of this point, a little to the east, it happened. All I saw was twelve inches of tail-clearing water. Then I saw Mister President striving with the rod. There was a terrible churning of water fifty feet out from the boat and there was the look of grim death on the face of the Old Man.

Then I saw that fish fling the bait and I felt the President of the Old

Duck Hunters land in my lap, for he had been bearing back and when the tension left the line he had to fall somewhere. Only quick footwork kept him from going overboard. He picked himself up and explained:

"Them you can't do a thing with. They make figure eights in one place the minute they feel steel. They just stand and grind the bait out of their face. If he'd have made a run for it and taken a couple champs at that bait — !"

Now I was excited.

But the Old Man was cool. "The big ones will take anything big that moves and looks like food," he declared. "They know that within a month they'll be living under the ice and the pickings may get slim. They're lardin' up."

"Eh?"

"Lardin' up, dang it! Putting on beef to take them through the winter."

"I'd rather hunt ducks."

"Row, you pup of a boy!"

The Old Man stuck with his job, no easy one. You have to know how to handle a half pound of bait on a 40-pound line. Heaving it forth is not so difficult, but the retrieve, giving it everything you have against the resistance of water, calls for strength as well as ingenuity. Once I climbed twelve feet up in a shore tamarack to fetch down the sacred bait when he had snapped it too fast on the heave and the line broke.

"We'll get one," he insisted. "They're lardin' up."

"I love the taste of duck — wild rice, turnnips, mashed potatoes, currant jam...."

"Son, when I hanker for a muskie, I hanker!"

I rowed. I rowed along the west shore of Lyman Lake until my arms ached. It went on for hours. The wind came up from the west, and I had to keep jockeying Jerry's 300-pound tub to hold the Old Man within casting range of the shallows. It was after the noon hour under that dark November sky when he suddenly snapped: "Back up!"

I had seen nothing. Truth is, I was so bored with the whole business that I wished I had gone duck hunting on a solo expedition. I pushed back on the oars, and the old tub responded sluggishly. He whispered, "Back up, son, or I'll scream!"

Then he said: "Wo-o-op! Stop 'er! He was off that bog — followed the bait out ten feet."

Time and again he flung out the water-soaked cedar toward the bog. He

[153]

explained, "This'n wasn't just a follower. He was nervous. He didn't put his nose on the bait like a summer muskie and follow it back to the boat. He came with a dash. He meant business. He's like the rest, lardin' up."

I didn't even hear the surface splash which he later said marked the appearance of a pair of jaws and the disappearance of his cedar plug. But I certainly heard the orders from the poop-deck: "Row like blazes out of here. This'n has got it good!"

I rowed and he manipulated. It was tame at first. The fish was heavy, but he was tractable. He came along nicely as I rowed for deep water. Once there, the Old Man decided it was time to put on the pressure. He cranked in ten feet of line, and a blotch of olive, blended with lake spray, went up in the air four feet.

It is not for me to say that the area was blessed with fair language from Mister President. I am a reporter. But I can say for publication that after the fish's fourth mad, shaking jump the Old Man, dogging him as he went down, turned and said: "Old Dynamite Joe himself! If he jumps once more, he may shake out the hooks."

He did jump again, and once again, in the wild, crazy way that muskies resent capture, but Mister President saw the jumps coming and slacked off with line so that the fish jumped against nothing. The Old Duck Hunters' Association took that muskie a good half mile in the wind and waves. The Old Man alternately stood up and sat down as the tide of battle rose and fell. I had no idea how big the fish went; just knew he was heavy by the way Hizzoner brought up his left hand to support the high joint on his old-fashioned muskie rod.

He led that November lightning bolt to his end. He worked him alongside, took a look, let him run again, and said: "When I fetch him sidewise again, tip the boat 'til she ships water. We'll float him in!"

Alongside came the muskie, docile yet dangerous. I leaned hard on the starboard gunwale of Jerry's logy tub. Water poured over it, a lot of water, and then a hell of a lot of fish as Mister President led him around it.

The Old Man dropped his rod and fell on the fish. He fell on him toward the rear. We had shipped a good two inches of Lyman Lake; so all I saw for awhile was fish, spray and the back of the old mackinaw as the President of the Old Duck Hunters clinched the victory. He literally climbed up that muskie's frame from the tail to the head to hold him down, then subdued him with a piece of broken rowboat seat.

Later Jerry's scales read 25 pounds, but all pride vanished when Jerry said that the week before "A railroad detective on vacation took two, both over 30 pounds."

We tried again. The Old Man rowed all over the lake for me while I heaved his whittled bait. Nothing came of it, and toward later afternoon he permitted himself to succumb to ducks. We set up on the bog at the sound end of Lyman where there was plenty of popple and birch overhead. We spread his single sack of decoys. There was just one gun between us.

I missed a brace of whistlers and said I thought they were pretty far out — "Maybe I should have let them go by." He snatched the automatic from me, jammed in shells and shot almost straight up through tree branches. A pair of black ducks thumped down in a shower of twigs. He asked. "What'd you say about them whistlers?"

"Nuts to you," I answered.

We rowed back to Jerry's. He said, as I plied the oars, "A fine fish. She'll bake it and invite all the neighbors."

He stretched back and took it easy, and at Jerry's reminded me not to turn down those white buckskin chopper's mitts. I had three pairs of them home as it was, and said so. He said he had seven pairs and that I'd better buy my fourth pair! I certainly did.

I admired the fish, lying on newspapers in the car, as we prepared to leave. The Old Man tarried for a word with Jerry. He told Jerry that I was skeptical about it all. He said, "Jerry, don't they lard up in the fall!"

Jerry answered: "You mean he figgers a fish would try to go through the winter without no ballast?"

One of the loveable traits of Mr. President is that he is an unabashed shirker. Mysterious aches and pains plague him when the time comes for heavy rowing or, in this case, poling a canoe upstream. The reason we forgive him goes back to those more important qualities — his humor, his decency, his sense of fun and ability to enjoy, the fact that MacQuarrie would gladly do all the poling to share the older man's company.

Finally, everyone knows that when and if the Old Man's ability is ever needed, he'll be there giving one hundred percent.

Hit The Drink

The President of the Old Duck Hunters' Association, Inc., softly closed his back door and came down the steps in the near dark to stow a last armload of gear into the car. A match flared as he relit the battered brier, and from the top of a telephone pole came the triumphant morning music of a robin.

"Listen!" the old man whispered.

He got in the seat beside me, closed the car door without slamming it, cranked down a window, and cocked an ear. By the very faint outdoors light and some light from the instrument board I watched Mister President. His eyes crinkled at the corners as the lone robin sang of mysterious and wonderful things in which he would take part on this, the first day of May.

The President whispered: "That guy is the first one up every morning. He gets the tallest pole. Likes to hear himself sing — like a man in a bathtub."

The soloist on the pole was making music from a full heart and a full stomach. Obviously he sang of a fine world for living in, with acres of lawns and plenty of worms. He seemed carried into ecstasy with the wonder of it all, for at times there was too much music in him to come out of one robin throat. Then he sounded like two robins. This made the Old Man grin all the more.

The singer on the pole still had the stage to himself when I backed the car down the driveway and headed east. Other autos were on the go, all rolling east from the head of Lake Superior to scores of trout streams which emerge in the north Wisconsin highland and run down to the greatest of fresh-water lakes.

Mister President pulled his old brown mackinaw about him and tended the battered brier.

"That robin on the pole," he mused. "The beggar can sing, but he won't work. You think he helped me dig worms last night? No, sir! He came around after I finished and gobbled up the little ones I left. Ah, dear. When a man's in love he'll stop at nothing."

Daylight built up slowly. There were scores of cars on the road, all of them with trout fishermen, many of them driving a little madly as is the way on opening day. We were in no hurry. Johnny Degerman had reserved our canoe. We passed through sleeping hamlets where windows were lit — more fishermen gulping breakfast.

Beyond the village of Lake Nebagamon we went straight south over a crooked gravel road to Stone's Bridge on the upper Brule River. We were the first at the dock, as Johnny had guessed we would be. He had left a scribbled note on the bow chair of the canoe riding at the downstream end of a flotilla of twenty: "Mac, take this one."

Mister President rigged his rod with the long grip while I loaded the canoe. It was fairly light as we shoved off, but there was no sign of the sun yet. The Brule took charge of the canoe, and we were off, the Old Man's snaky brown line swishing over my head like the call of distant whippoorwills. The Old Duck Hunters' Association fishes this river by ritual: the old Man in the bow chair an hour, I in the stern with pole and paddle; then switch over for the next hour.

There is big magic in this lovely river, and never more than just before sunup of opening day. The brethren who have learned to love this stream will know how it can be.

Winter done. Waxwings murmuring in the cedars. The Brule sucking around the rocks. Dabs of fog rising here and there. A woodpecker hammering a rampike. The Bois Brule winding at the bottom of its deep valley, saying, "I've got 'em if you're man enough to take 'em from me."

We were not out of sight of Stone's Bridge when the Old Man's single wet coachman had found a good native brook about a foot long. It tore out from beneath brush and logs. I netted it and dropped it through the slot in the door of the live-well.

As is often the case on this river, Mister President was plagued with small rainbows. They are pugnacious, undersized busters willing to have a go at almost anything offered. These ridiculous midgets, thick in the belly, averaging five to six inches long, grab flies as large as No. 8's, then fling themselves hither and yon, as though they can lick the world and everything in it.

We put the bridge behind us around the first bend and went on down between alders. The stream narrows here to about twenty feet in width, with deep water at the left bank where the alder tips trail. Mister President nailed another native — a typical dark-bodied, red-bellied Brule "sped," not smart like a brown, but bursting with vitality.

A half mile from the bridge we knew the sun was up but that it would be awhile yet before it crept over the Norways on the high hills to flood the river. Mister President broached an idea; "Let's shove on down fast for two good miles, just in case somebody from the bridge has the same idea."

For half an hour we poled together, putting distance behind and passing up beautiful stretches of fly water. Never mind, there will be plenty of such good water down below. Yet it's not an easy thing to pole when trout are dimpling. Then the hand itches for the feel of cork.

Below the Buckhorn, a luncheon ground marked by antlers nailed to a tree, Mister President went at it again. He feared that no lunker rainbows would be so far upstream. The spawning run had been early. So he retained his light leader.

To be sure, it happened, it always does. In a place where the Brule spreads out over washed gravel, a rainbow of about four pounds offered battle. It was all over in something like six seconds. The fish shot off the shoal to deep water, plunged downstream in the main current — and that's all there was to it.

"Somebody in this organization," Mister President wailed, "had ought to fine me about $10,000."

"Put on a leader. There are a few big ones here anyway. I know a place."

He rerigged while I poled to the next likely spot for a big one. Brule rainbows are great ones for lying over gravel beds in pretty swift current. I have seen scores of them lying so, up to 10 pounds and better, in areas so restricted that they scrap among themselves for elbow-room.

The Old Man dug up a bass leader and with a dark bass-sized bucktail, good Brule medicine on big fish, flailed the water. He failed to get a roll and his hour was up, so we exchanged places. I was using Mr. President's

outfit. He let the canoe work down to the end of this gravel bed.

Wham! A fine word, that for rainbows. This fellow did as all smart rainbows do — work into the current, lie in it crosswise, then jerk, jerk, jerk! They have plenty of power and they know how to let the current add to it. I pinned my hopes on that bass leader. When the fish broke, he looked pretty good, deep in the middle. As soon as Mister President saw him he ordered: "Hit the drink!"

Overboard the water was cold as sin. The Old Man knew what he was doing when he shouted that advice. He knew that a wading fisherman had more maneuverability than one in the most skillfully handled boat. The rainbow took me downstream about fifty yards. Once off the gravel bed there were holes to contend with, some of them right against the bank. Sometimes I got through them only by hanging to cedar boughs. Mister President followed in the canoe.

The rainbow gave me hell in more ways than one. Not the least of it was the cold of the river. The fish just decided: "If you're going to fight me, you do it on my home grounds."

When the jerking had subsided, I heard a splashing behind me. It was the Old Man in there with me, belly-deep. No waders. He was busy unwinding the white cotton mesh of a four-foot net as he waded below me and below the sulking fish. He did not miss on the first pass. Slabsides went to his destiny in the long white meshes.

The two of us got ashore and made a fire. We had to open the live-well cover to put the big rainbow inside. He was too much fish to go through the slot. We stripped before the fire and dried out. The sun had finally found the bottom of the valley. It felt mighty good. We boiled coffee and fried the two brookies.

If you ever get to fish the Brule, bring along a little bacon, some fresh home-made bread and a chunk of butter. And a frying-pan.

It came Mister President's turn to regain the bow chair. The sun was high and the day warm. He returned to a light leader and small wet flies. Under such conditions he swears by such as Cowdungs, Hare's Ears, Brown Hackles.

He picked up some small native and a few fly-weight rainbows, and so did I when it came my turn to ride the prow chair. These went into the live-well where Slabsides announced his living presence every whipstitch by banging his prison wall with a broad tail. It's good to hear them thump like that.

After the noon hour Mister President announced, "We'll go ashore here."

The Old Duck Hunters always go ashore at this place, which is May's Rips, six miles downstream from the put-in bridge. It's a place where the Brule is beginning to feel its oats and starting to make some downhill jumps on its way to Gitche Gumee.

"I can eat 'em twice a day, and then some," said Mister President, busy with the skillet.

We dried our clothes some more. We spread a couple of blankets on a cedar knoll and lazily watched other canoes, with other fishermen, come down the waters which we had explored first in the season. We listened to the croaks of wheeling ravens and the talk of the river elbowing down through May's Rips, and also we listened to the dear music of the white-throated sparrow, which sounds so sad and makes trout fishermen so happy.

We dozed. Mister President was snoring when I awoke. He aroused slowly.

"Dammit!" he said. "I got a crick in my left shoulder. Dunno as I'll be much good poling back upstream."

There was evidence that the three hours of repose had stiffened his shoulder. It seemed the ground damp had come right up though the blanket.

"But my right shoulder's all right," he observed.

"You can swing a fly rod?"

"It'll hurt, but I can do it."

I took over the poling and he seized the bamboo scepter and moved in to the throne in the bow. Now it was upstream fishing with floating flies. The time of day was excellent for such business. It had been warm enough to produce a sustained hatch of gray-blue fliers, lots of them. A brown bivisible, size 12, did the trick. A good number of pan-warmers joined Slabsides in his captivity in the live-well.

"But there ain't much to show the neighbors except that rainbow," Mister President pointed out.

In one still, deep pool the Old Man bit through the gut, stuck the floater in his hat-band and dunked with worms shamelessly and successfully for browns which would not surface. He took three. One, he insisted, would "go pound and a half on our butcher's scale."

Upper Brule browns in those deep holes are challengers. There are plen-

[164]

ty of them, all very sharp-witted, or cautious, which amounts to the same thing for a fish. Given a dark, warm, windy day over these holes, a man has a fair chance to show them who's boss. On 'most any other kind of day they just lie there and snicker at you.

The shadows of the cedars on the river stretched out. Clouds riding a southwest wind formed blackly. Nighthawks swooped. It would rain before we made Stone's Bridge. Mister President put on his mackinaw and kept fishing. The rain stabbed violently at the Brule.

In ten minutes it was over and the nighthawks were diving once more. The sun came out strong. A porky swam the stream, floating high. The rain made everything smell good. Mister President loosened the single button on his mackinaw and shook it to throw off the rain drops. He said, "My left shoulder is pretty creaky."

I poled on upstream and he dozed in the sun. From my place in the stern I could see more of the gray of his hair as his head fell forward. Slab-sides thumped in the live-well.

My hand itched for cork, as fish were rising. But it would not be the right thing to wake up the Old Man. The Old Duck Hunters' junior membership opposes such nonsense.

There is a place about a mile and a half below Stone's Bridge where the Brule twists and narrows among rocks and captured logs and brush. It was here where the itching rod hand became too much to ignore. I crawled forward and got the rod, crawled back to the stern and worked paddle and rod together, which takes some doing, unless you are of a piece with some Brules guides, which I am not.

A good fish was feeding boldly on the left bank, right under the brush. I managed to keep the canoe in position long enough to lay one good one in the right spot above him. It floated down. He just walked over and sucked it in. I dropped the paddle and let the canoe do what it would.

That brown was not more than a two-pounder. But he put a set in the rod on his first dash. It is not easy to handle a canoe and a brown at once in quick current. Luck and good tackle held him. He went under the canoe and then downstream while the canoe yawed in the current.

"Hit the drink!" It was the Old Man, suddenly awake, yelling good advice again. In I went. The water seemed just as cold. And downstream went Mister Brown to a snaggy hole below a small rapids.

This time the President of the Old Duck Hunters' Association did not join me. He did the entire job of coaching from the bow-chair throne.

Sometimes he cussed a little, as when I let the fish get in under the bank. He hung on to cedar branches to keep the canoe from drifting down on top of the battle. Then he flung the net to me, and I grabbed its floating wood handle as it went by.

So eventually I came dripping back into the canoe with a nice fish and a badly set tip joint on a grand old trout rod. Mister President had the cover of the live-well wide open for me. He looked in on the welter of trout there. Then he took out his "gold watch and chain" and noted the time. He said we could just make it back to Stone's Bridge before dark if he poled — in the stern.

Unloading at the bridge I asked him, "How come you could pole up a mile and a half of current with that sore shoulder?"

"Sore shoulder? Oh, that. Funny the way them aches and pains come and go."

"I was beginning to think golf is a pretty good game after all, considering the shower bath that goes with it." Pure MacQuarrie. His humor works because it is effortless. He just slides it in.

Here is another of MacQuarrie's themes, this as most, put forth by Hizzoner. Old things are better than new things. Old time flies. Old decoys. Old waders and hats and the old brown Mackinaw with one button at the top and an alarm clock that runs only when stood on its face. And, of course, one — no two — incomparable.

Them Old Time Flies

The Brule River of Wisconsin lay fifteen miles out of my way, but I drove to it anyway, like a swain to his true love. The look of it disappointed me. Standing on the Winnebojou wagon bridge, I felt that the river was off form.

I can hardly explain why I felt that way. Perhaps it was the absence of rising trout, or the recollection of the prolonged hot spell which, even as I stood there studying the current, sent sweat down my neck. Or it might have been the long summer water plants streaming from the Brule's bottom in places.

I'm making a mess out of trying to explain something I cannot rightly explain. To make certain of my hunch, I diverged farther from my route and inspected the river from other points, including Stone's bridge, which spans the upper river a good forty-five miles from Lake Superior, as the river goes.

This place seldom fails to quicken my pulse, which is the way things are between the Brule and me. There have been times at this old putting-in place when, in a canoe with trout rising, I have missed a guide or two in my rod while stringing up. This particular evening it left me cold. Maybe it didn't look right because I couldn't remain and fish it, even if I had wanted to. There was work to do in other places. Who can say how much of a fisherman's judgment depends upon his own state of mind? And how much of his success?

It was late in August the next time I braked down the Winnebojou hill and leaned over the steel bridge rail to look again upon this lovely river. So help me, it looked right! Actually, it seemed no different. The same cold, ropey water came around the bend and whispered under the bridge. The same whippoorwills were making the same old music. The same absence of rising trout was noted. But it looked right.

Gentlemen, you may hang, draw and quarter me, but I can contribute no more to the angler's relentless pursuit of cause and effect than to say the stream looked right. I have seen other fishermen in such throes — certain they would be successful, but not able to explain their confidence. I remember an evening on the Brule at quitting time years ago. Carl Miller, a guide, was standing on Stone's bridge gloomily studying the water. It was the end of a poor day of fishing. "She won't be worth a darn for three days," he said. "Come back then." He didn't know why. It turned out subsequently that he was correct.

So, with a feeling that the augur was good, I drove along — up Johnny Degerman's hill toward the vast, sad pine barrens which feed their rainfall to the Brule, and came eventually to a low-lying log cabin where a light gleamed. There, beneath the light, the President of the Old Duck Hunters' Association, Inc., sat reading a two-week-old newspaper.

"Thought you'd drop by on the way north," he greeted. "Where you been?"

"Never mind, sir. Have you caught any trout?"

"The Brule hasn't been right."

It turned out that he had "a hatful of trout," taken from a creek of minor distinction called Long Branch. They tasted so good that I washed and wiped the dishes. We sat, talking.

"She looked right when I passed by," I said

"Been pretty warm."

"Nights are cooler and longer," I pressed.

"If you've got a full day, we could slip down to the Chippewa flowage and show our collection of big hardware to the muskies."

"How cool was it when you got up this morning?"

"Forty-one at 6 A.M."

"Been cool right along — nights?"

"Two blankets."

"We'll fish the Brule, your Honor!"

The Old Man tamped new tobacco over old in his crooked pipe. "We could get us some bass. Drift from the iron bridge on the Namakagon down to the St. Croix. Get Jens to pick up out at nine."

"She looked right to me, I tell you."

"Oh, the Brule. Hm-m-m. How about us getting a half dozen big suckers and lacing the flowage for one big muskie?"

"Mister President," I said, rather sharply, considering my junior membership in the Association, "why don't you want to fish the Bois Brule when I say she looks right, and when there are only ten days left of the season?"

He came clean: "Dang it to blazes! I lost my fly-book on Long Branch, that derned, ornery, deep-valleyed, wood-tick-ridden drainage ditch!"

This was serious. Mister President's fly-book was a fly-book! It was three inches thick, loaded with trout flies which had become for him precious talismen in thirty-five years of filling it with lies. A thing with a tattered leather cover, worn but efficient. It hurt to know it was gone.

"I have with me at least four hundred flies," I offered.

"Not my kind of flies."

I had him cold there. I went to my car and produced an aluminum box in which were stored only flies which he had given me over a period of twenty years. I spilled them out on the table, explaining where I had got them. His eyes brightened as he saw beneath the table lamp the dull maroon of ancient ragged Montreals, the brazen red of Parmacheene Belles, the silvery blue of Silver Doctors.

In that noble old collection, some of which had seen thirty years of service, were wet flies in the great old tradition — bright McGintys, plain and Royal Coachmen, Cowdungs, Seth Greens, Grizzly Kings, Brown Hackles, Black Gnats — all the common, proven wet flies which Mister President had learned to trust through performance. It seemed to me then that he might rejoice. Instead he chose to drive a point, the while scooping up the antiques and restoring them to their compartments.

"Right there's all the flies a man needs. What's come over this new generation of fishermen? They've got to have something new every whipstitch. I know people tying flies who never went fishing in their lives. Yes, sir! They take it up like women take up needlework — and make flies for hatbands, not for fishing. Imagine!

"And what sort fo flies?" He rose to magnificent oratory. "The goldangedst, no-name, hybrid, sloppy-hackled flies imaginable. You know what" — shaking a finger under my nose — "there was a time when a hundred patterns of flies were known and proven. Today there are ten thousand!"

"You don't have to use them, your honor."

"And I ain't gonna!"

He fingered the box, sort of caressing it, and I thought again he would mellow, but he continued: "I've got no quarrel with new fangled flies if they deliver the goods. What I object to are non-fishing amateurs twisting up flies like so many idiots because they like the colors." He fairly snorted. "Why, lots of them are using neck hackle from old brokendown hens that should have been pensioned instead of plucked!"

I reminded him that there had been some splendid developments in fly-rod lures these last twenty-five years — nymphs, bivisibles, new streamers, spiders, fanwings. He agreed grudgingly, patted the box of old flies, wound his six-ounce gold watch deliberately and went to bed, calling: "Set the alarm for 2:30. We've got twenty miles to drive."

It was certainly a chilly morning, such a one as the north can turn up in late August to make a man think of hunting to come. In the night I had dragged two blankets over me. The alarm petered out, and its dying sound was joined, then replaced by the clank of the kitchen pump. As usual, Mister President had beat the clock. He was in his waders and brogues. "Might as well put 'em on. It's a cold morning, and we'll save time when we get there by wearing 'em."

Mister President nursed his heavy old car deliberately and carefully down the narrow trail between the pine trees. The pre-dawn deer were abroad, standing in the glare of the lamps so that twice Mister President had to apply the brakes. Snowshoe rabbits darted across the road. At one inroad where we stopped to reconnoiter Mister President swished a bush with his foot and heavy dew flashed.

"Two degrees lower, and we'd have had a frost," he remarked.

The place where we stopped, after some debate, was not the spot twenty miles distant to which we first planned going. This place was thirty miles away from our starting-point, attained by a road to the lower Brule, over hogback clay hills, not more than a few miles from Lake Superior. Hizzoner turned the car into a small meadow, and by the car lights we saw that frost had barely brushed the grass tops.

"Bet those waders feel good now," said Mister President. "Frosts every month of the year down here." He had insisted on this lower reach of river "because there'll be some early browns from the lake working in. Might even hook a rainbow, though it's early for that."

The Brule and many other mid-Western streams produce rainbow runs at the end of summer. Little is known about these runs. The big runs of rainbows are in the spring.

Before he departed downstream he held the box of ancient flies to the brightening eastern sky, with the cover open, as though to assure himself that these were the same friends of his younger days. Ordinarily at this place I go upstream from a wooden bridge. I like upstream fishing, wet or dry, on the Brule or any place.

This morning, with Mister President's warning of possible browns in from Lake Superior, I went downstream, but not with the Old Man. It never does for a fisherman of this Association to follow another one, stepping on his heels. Anyway, not at the beginning of the day. Later, when sociability becomes more important than trout, the members of this Association customarily make a rendezvous and fish together. Mister President is a downstream man by habit, a product of the wet-fly days.

I walked up two of the clay hogbacks and struck north, through brush, to get below Mister President. The going was bad — heavy spruce in low places, endless popple and hazel on higher lands. After the battle with the brush, it was a relief to slip into the Brule at a wide spot and sort of lean back against the current. It had been so cold in the night that the mosquitoes were dormant. Ramparts of spruce leaned on the right bank, with here and there a solitary cork pine.

Within five minutes Mister President's hunch about Gitche Gumee browns came true. One grabbed my wet squirrel-tail streamer, darted sidewise in heavy current and snapped the 3x leader as easily as that. I put on a heavier leader with the same pattern of streamer, and the second one did not get away. He went about a pound and a half and felt very good as he shaped to the 16-inch width of my fish pocket. This, I decided, was going to be easy.

A half hour later, with nothing more in the fish pocket, I reminded myself what the Old Man would have said, had he been there: "Pride goeth before fall, and right after fall you get a long, hard winter."

I tried spinners and combinations with flies. I turned around and faced the current, floating flies and dunking them. The sun got above the horizon and lit up the tops of the spruces. A few of the hardier mosquitoes punched the clock and manned their drills. A little wind came blowing against the northwest. Partridge drummed. The Brule mocked me.

In desperation I turned downstream again, biting off gut and replacing flies until I remembered what the Old Man had said one day: "Son you're gonna wear down your front teeth on silk-worm gut," and then he calmly bit through his own heavy leader and changed his fly.

The Brule has often whipped me — much more often than it has suddenly turned into a place I felt was the world with a fence around it and full of trout. This odd river does this to me at just about the time I begin to think golf is a pretty good game after all, considering the shower-bath that goes with it.

The fly that did it was a soft-hackled monstrosity on a long-shank hook. No name for it. Just something somebody tied up. Like most trout fishermen, I have traded flies with the brethren from coast to coast. It's a good custom, indicative of the fraternity that prevails among men who fish trout. The predominant colors of this nondescript were purple, and yellow, and the minute it hit the surface its soft hackle subsided so that, drawn through the water, it was just a streak of color.

You have seen flies like this, often tied by local amateurs, in hatbands, clipped to cardboard sales displays, and perhaps speared through the corner of a letter to you from some hopeful who writes: "Give it a try and let me know." The hook on which it was tied was thin, but it wasn't brittle. It bent some on the second solidly hooked brown, and it bent on the third and fourth and the fifth, so that each time I'd have to straighten it a little. And each time I straightened it and looked at its complete lack of distinction I had to say: "I'll be damned!"

I don't know why they went for that funny fly any more than I know why the Brule looked good to me the evening before. Every fish it took was a brown; one went close to two pounds. They felt good as I went back upstream through the streamside brush, sweating. It would be another hot day. None but those who had been there at 3:30 A.M. could believe that frost had kissed the lower Brule bottoms a few hours before.

In the mile and a half of water I passed going back I did not find Mister President, or anyone else. I got all the way back to the car in the meadow and looked across the current. The car doors were closed. No rod leaned against it. Where was Mister President? I was about to wade the river when he emerged from the spruce at the edge of the meadow.

Carrying a World War I trench shovel under his arm, he peered into and poked at a red tobacco tin as he walked. He stowed the shovel in the car trunk, hitched up his patched waders, took his rod from where it leaned against a lone spruce at the river's edge and glided along the Brule's right

bank, downstream. I knew exactly where he was going, to a place called McNeil's Pool.

With angleworms! Ah, the old flies, the good old proven killers. Can you blame me for laughing out loud as I waded the Brule to the car? Can you blame me for chuckling as I got out of my waders? As the Old Man came striding out of the spruce with the shovel and the worm can he looked exactly like a fellow who has said to himself: "Well, boys, here is where all friendship ceases. I am now going to put on a pair of brass knuckles and take the joint apart!"

I put my gear away and let down the car windows. The wind was strong enough to discourage the deer flies, so I dozed. It was near noon when the car door opened and Mister President yelled, "Ro-o-o-l out, you whelp of a boy, and have a look at some old-time trout caught with old-time flies!"

He laid before me on the grass a creelful of magnificent browns, topped by one three-pound rainbow, a pale hard-fleshed thing which might have been a steelhead, but we won't go into that here.

He was simply jubilant. "Reminds me of the old days," he said, "when Fred and I used to take our limits of brooks in an hour — on those old-time flies, son. You can't beat 'em."

I showed him my fish. He felt so good about everything that he did not even sneer at them. He said, "Mighty nice pan-fish there, son, mighty nice."

On the way back to the shack he got off about four moralistic sermons on the virtues of old-time flies, in such language as would have done credit to Chautauqua's greatest spellbinders, including Bill Bryan. He was tired; so I toted the gear from the car down the hill to the place. While he stretched out on a couch I scrubbed the new potatoes, made the salad, brewed the tea and did up four trout in deep fat.

All through the meal he regaled me with the morning's events: "You take that dark Montreal and let 'er sink, retrieving with slow jerks — nothing better...As for a Silver Doctor, I like it out in midstream, where the water's fast...Might be they think it's a minnie...."

While I washed the dishes he kept it up. I heard the history of the old-time flies told and retold. "You take that Tom Bosworth, tied the plain Coachman. Used to drive for Queen Victoria. Could flick a pipe out of the mouth of a man with his whip as he drove the old lady around London...Must have been a piece of a man."

He fell asleep on the couch, and I straightened up our gear. As I picked up his fishing jacket from the heap on the floor, the red tin tobacco can fell from a pocket. It was empty. Bits of fresh dried earth clung to it. I set it on the mantelpiece and finished straightening things up. Then I placed the empty tin on a card table, beside the Old Man's couch, with a sign penciled on cardboard: "Them Old-Time Flies."

He awoke around four in the afternoon, yawned, stretched, looked at his watch, saw the display and chuckled.

"You can't beat 'em! How 'bout you and me getting in a little bass fishing 'fore dark?"

"Surely He shall deliver thee from the snare of the fowler." More hi-jinks coming up. Mr. President is outfoxing other hunters which always brings out the best (or the worst!) in him. This is bad enough but where MacQuarrie got the idea for the biblical quotes, I can't imagine. Somebody that used them must have inspire him. With a book of biblical quotes by his side he put the ODHA into action enjoying himself immensely.

In The Presence
Of Mine Enemies

The dusk of late duck season was
hurrying westward across the sky and slanting snow was whitening the
street gutters as I turned into the automotive emporium of the President
of the Old Duck Hunters' Association, Inc. The man in the parts depart-
ment explained that Hizzoner was out on the used-car lot. There I found
him, thoughtfully kicking a tire on an august and monstrous second-hand
car, soon to be taking the Association on its final expedition of the season.

"We could try Libby Bay again," he reflected. "But the Hole in the Wall
will be frozen. Jens says every bluebill on Dig Devil's has hauled his
freight. Shallow Bay'd be open at the narrows, but I s'pose Joe's hauled
in all his boats. Phoned Hank. He said there's an inch of ice on Mud Lake
and she's making fast."

He went over other possibilities. The situation was urgent, for only a
few days remained of the season. The widespread below the Copper Dam
on the St. Croix? "Might not see a thing 'cept sawbills." The grassy island
in the open water of the St. Louis River? "Too much big water to buck in
this wind." Taylor's Point on the Big Eau Claire? "Wind's wrong for it
and she's gonna stay in that quarter."

Street lights came on and home-going city toilers bent into the growing
storm with collars turned up. One of them crossed the street and tried the
showroom door which the parts man had just locked. Mister President
called from the lot, "Something I can do for you?"

"Ye're dern tootin'!" came the reply. "Open up this dump and let a man

[179]

get warm."

Mister President grinned. "It's Chad," he said, making haste to unlock the showroom door.

Anyone in that community on reasonable terms with the way of the duck, the trout, the partridge and the white-tailed deer knows Chad just as he knows Mister President. Before the days when I cut myself in as an apprentice, the ODHA had consisted almost solely of Mister President and Chad. In recent years they get together only a couple of times per year on outdoor missions which can be anything from looking up old trout holes to picking blueberries.

But they meet regularly in church, except during the duck season and possibly two or three Sundays in late May or early June when the shad-flies hatch. Chad is an especially stout pillar of the church, and passes the collection plate with a stern and challenging eye on the brethren he considers too thrifty.

The belligerent affection which Hizzoner and Chad reciprocate was once amply demonstrated at a Men's Club meeting in the church basement when suggestions were called for.

"Get a one-armed guy to take Chad's job passing the plate," volunteered Mister President.

Chad, who came upon holiness late in life and became so enchanted with Biblical wisdom that he quotes verses every chance, snorted back, "Let him who is without sin cast the first stone..."

"The time," Chad announced, "is short."

"There'll be no 14-year-old touring car with California top repaired here this night," declared Mister President. "Tell you what, though — bring it down to the lot and I'll give you $7.50 for it on a new job."

"My son, attend unto my wisdom," said Chad sagely. "Last deer season I was on a drive in back of Little Bass Lake. Found a spring-hole at the edge of a big marsh." His eyes gleamed with what is recognized in church as religious fervor. "No map shows it. Everything else in the country was froze up, and this little spring-hole was open. There's a point of high, dry land poking into it. There's smartweed in there and watercress, and the day I saw it mallards jumped out of it."

"How about the road in?"

"We'll have to walk a mile."

Mister President frowned briefly, but Chad's mustache became a reasonable straight line as he intoned, "If thou faint in the day of adversity, thy strength is small."

"Let's at it, then," decided Mister President.

Quick getaways are no problem for the ODHA in the critical times of the season. At such times decoys are always sorted and sacked, shell boxes full and thermos bottles yawning for their soup and coffee. Against emergency conditions, Mister President also sets the old horse blanket and barn lantern conveniently at hand in the garage, for it is by these implements that he keeps warm in late-season blinds.

A mere accessory to their reunion, I drove the big car while the two cronies smoked and remembered. They agreed I'd come in handy toting gear and that I could be put to use if ice had to be broken. Objections on my part were swept away as Chad patted me on the back and said piously, "The righteous shall flourish like the palm tree."

Fine slanting snow darted across the path of the headlights. With that northwest wind I knew it would not snow much; but should the wind veer to the northeast, then we would be very happy at having the heavy, high-wheeled monster of a car for bucking drifts. It was a little after 9 P.M. when we disembarked beneath the high oaks which spread over Norm's place on the north shore of Big Yellow Lake, Burnett County, Wisconsin. Norm appeared with a flashlight.

"Might have known it'd be no one but you out on a night like this."

He lit an air-tight stove in an overnight cabin. Chad, police suspenders drooping as he readied for bed, set his old alarm clock with the bell on top for 5 A.M. A few minutes were allowed for final smokes and for further recollection of past delights. Chad had started to recall "the night we slept on the depot floor at Winnebojou" when a car entered the yard.

Again Norm emerged, prepared a cabin, and went back to sleep. As is always the way in duck camps, the newcomers pounded on our door for a pre-dawn investigation. As the two men entered, somewhat suspiciously I thought, Chad's face fell for a brief instant, but he made a quick recovery and fell upon the two hunters with vast friendship.

Where were they going to hunt in the morning? Weren't we all crazy for being out in such weather? How's the missus and the children?

Chad volunteered with bare-faced frankness that we were "going down the Yellow River a piece to that widespread just this side of Eastman's." Our visitors alleged they had it in mind to try the deep point in the cane grass across Big Yellow. Mister President and Chad solemnly agreed that sounded like a promising spot — "mighty promising."

[181]

The two departed for bed, and Chad cried after them cheerfully, "See you in church, boys!" The moment they were gone Chad seized his alarm clock and set it to ring an hour earlier. "Those fakers aren't fooling me," he snorted.

"Me, either," said Mister President. "Somebody knows something."

"They were with me on that deer drive last fall. Gentlemen, say your prayers well tonight. There's only one spot on that marsh that's really any good, and that's the little spring-hole." He rolled in with a final muttering: "Deliver me from the workers of iniquity."

Within a few minutes the cabin resounded with the devout snores of Mister President and Chad. I lay awake a bit longer, listening to the wind in the oaks, weighing our chances for the morrow and marveling at the hypocritical poise of my comrades in the face of emergency. I knew those two adversaries of ours better than well. One was a piano tuner who, by some transference of vocational talent, could play a tune on a Model '97 that was strictly lethal so far as ducks are concerned. The other was a butcher likewise noted for his wing-shooting and his stoutness in going anywhere after ducks.

Mister President and Chad snored. The snow tapped on the window like fine sand, and then suddenly someone was shaking me in the dark. It was Mister President.

"Get up quietly," he hissed. "We beat the alarm clock so they wouldn't hear it. Don't turn on the light. Don't even strike a match!"

Like burglars we groped in the dark getting dressed and gathering up gear. "How about breakfast?" I asked. Mister President snickered, and Chad's voice came as from a sepulcher in the pitch dark: "Trust in the Lord and do good."

Softly we closed the door behind us and climbed into the car. Mister President got behind the wheel with Chad beside him and me alone in the back seat. The motor roared, headlights blazed and almost simultaneously a light went on in the cabin of our neighbors.

"Step on 'er!" Chad shouted, and the old crate made the snow fly as it leaped out of Norm's yard.

"We've got the jump on 'em," Chad exulted, but did not forget to add: "The righteous shall inherit the land and dwell forever."

It was a wild ride on a wild morning. The snow had stopped when two to three inches lay on the level. That was enough to make for skidding turns on the sharp corners where Mister President kept to maximum speed. We roared up steep hills and kept the power on going down. We passed white barns ghostly and cold-looking in the dark, and at a field fronting a farmstead owned by one honorary member of the ODHA, Gus Blomberg, Chad ordered the car halted. He got out, took something from Gus's front yard that rattled like tin and stuffed it into the car trunk.

"What was it, Chad?" I askd.

"Out of the mouths of babes and fools," he retaliated, poked Mister President in the ribs and roared: "Step on 'er some more! He shall deliver thee from the snare of the fowler!"

I knew part of the road. But after they skirted the base of the long point jutting into Little Bass Lake and took to pulp trails through the jack-pine barrens I was lost. Chad ordered "right," or "left," or sometimes, "Don't forget to turn out for that big scrub-oak."

We labored up a hilltop on a barely discernible pair of ruts, and the big car came to a stop, practically buried in low scrub-oak. Instantly the lights were switched off, and Mister President and Chad listened for sound of the enemy's motor. They heard nothing, but nevertheless hurried with the job of loading up with the sinews of war and heading for the spring-hole.

Only you who have been there know how a 60-pound sack of decoys in a Duluth pack-sack can cut into the shoulders when hands are occupied with gun and shellbox. Chad led the way in the dark and took us miraculously through the better parts of that oak and pine tangle. A half mile along the way we stopped to listen again, and this time we heard the motor of another car laboring up the hill through the scrub.

"Step on 'er again," counseled Chad, shouldering his burdens. "They haven't forgotten the way in, and that piano tuner can run like a deer!"

Chad permitted the use of lights now. We stumbled for what seemed miles until he led us down a gentle slope, and there before us was black, open water, about an acre of it. The omens were good. Mallards took off as a flashlight slit across the water.

"Keep the dang lights on all you want," said Mister President. "Let 'em know we're here fustest with the mostest."

Mister President and I spread his ancient decoys while Chad busied himself on a mysterious errand some distance away. As I uncoiled decoy strings I saw that the hole was a mere open dot in what must have been a large, flat marsh. Tall flaggers hemmed in the open water and stretched far beyond the range of the flashlight.

Mister President and I dug a pit in soft sand on fairly high ground and embroidered the edges of it with jack-pine and scrub-oak. We heard the piano tuner and the butcher push through the cover on the hill at our back, heard them panting and talking in low voices. Chad returned and boomed for all to hear: "Ain't a thing open but this one little patch. Betcha we don't see a feather here today!"

He fooled no one. The piano tuner and the butcher made a wide circle around us. We could hear them crashing through brush and Chad grudgingly allowed, "That butcher can hit the bush like a bull moose." Then we heard them walking across the marsh ice among the raspy flaggers and soon, five hundred yards across the marsh from us, came the sound of chopping as they readied a blind. Chad was worried.

"No open water there, but that's the place where the mallards come in here from the St. Croix River. Those muzzlers are right in front of a low pass through the hills. Them mallards come through there like you opened a door for 'em."

There was at least an hour's wait to shooting time. The two old hands puttered with the blind. They rigged crotched sticks to keep their shotgun breeches away from the dribbling sand of the blind's wall. They made comfortable seats for themselves, and finally, as was their right by seniority, they wrapped the old horse blanket about their knees, with the lantern beneath, and toasted their shins in stinking comfort.

Long before there was any real light, ducks returned to our open water, and the ODHA, waiting nervously, sipped coffee and made a career out of not clinking the aluminum cups. In that blind with Mister President it was almost worth a man's life to kick a shell-box accidentally in the dark.

Chad briefed us: "When the time comes, don't nobody miss on them first ones, 'cause our friends over there are situated to scare out incomers. That is, in case they get a shot. Praise be, neither one of them are cloudbusters."

As the zero hour approached Mister President produced his gold watch and chain, and the two of them followed the snail's pace of the minute hand.

"Good idea not to jump the gun," said Chad. "No use to break the law."

To which Mister President added: "Might be a game warden hanging around, too."

"Now!"

As Mister President gave the word Chad kicked his shell-box and stood up. The air was full of flailing wings. I missed one, got it with the second barrel and heard three calculated shots from Mister President's automatic. I also heard Chad's cussing. He had forgotten to load his cornsheller. The air was a bright cerulean blue until his city conscience smote him and he said remorsefully, "Wash me and I shall be whiter than snow."

With daylight the wind shifted from northwest to northeast and the snow began again, from Lake Superior this time. That kind of snow at that season is not to be trifled with, for northeasters can blow for three days and fetch mighty drifts. I picked up the drake mallard I had downed and the three birds Mister President had collected in his methodical way. The two old hands agreed that none of the mallards were locals, but "Redlegs down from Canada — feel the heft of that one!"

There was a long wait after that first burst of shooting. Obviously there were not many ducks left in the country. The original ODHA comforted themselves with hot coffee and thick sandwiches. From time to time one of them ascended the little knob at our rear to look across the snowy marsh and observe operations over there.

Chad came back from a reconnaissance and exclaimed, "She's workin', glory be."

The words were hardly out of his mouth when five mallard materialized out of the smother, circled the open water and cupped wings to drop in. As they zoomed in Mister President and Chad picked off a drake apiece, and when the wind had blown them to the edge of the ice I picked them up.

"You got him broke pretty well," Chad observed.

"Fair, just fair," grunted Mister President, squinting through the snow. "He's steady to wing and shot, but a mite nervous on incomers. Needs more field work."

Shortly before noon I climbed the hill myself for a look across the marsh. Through the snow over the high flaggers I could make out the dark green blob that was the jack-pine blind of the butcher and piano tuner. We had not heard a shot from the place. As l watched six mallards, mere specks at first, approached the marsh from the direction of the St. Croix River. They were coming through the low hill pass just as Chad had said they would. Normally they would have flown almost directly over the distant blind.

Some distance from the blind I saw them flare and climb, then swing wide around the edge of the marsh and sail straight into our open hole.

[186]

From my vantage-point I saw the two old hands rise and fire, and three ducks fell.

Mister President called up to me: "Pick up that one that dropped in the scrub, will yuh?"

"We'd better keep careful count," Chad suggested. In a few minutes he dropped two more that tried to sneak into the water-hole.

"I'm through," he announced. He acknowledged his limit with a thankful verse: "Thou hast turned for me my mourning into dancing."

The afternoon moved along. The snow increased, and when limits were had all around we finished the last of the soup, washed it down with the now luke-warm coffee and picked up. It was high time we were moving. A good six inches of snow was on the ground. There were steep, slippery hills between us and the main road.

Back at the car, we turned the behemoth around. Parked just to the rear of us was the conveyance of the piano tuner and the butcher. It was a modern job with the low-slung build of a dachshund, but in maneuvering out of the place Mister President's locomotive-like contraption broke out a good trail.

Mister President and Chad were jubilant as the big car was tooled carefully over the crooked road to Norm's where we picked up gear left behind in the unlighted cabin hours before and said goodby to Norm — "until the smallmouth take a notion to hit in the St. Croix."

Homeward-bound. Chad's best Sunday basso profundo broke into a sincere rendition of an old hymn which emphasizes that "He will carry you through," and Mister President joined him with a happy, off-key baritone. We halted at the curb in front of Chad's house, and he emerged from the car laden with mallards and gear and smelling of horse blanket and kerosene.

"We sure fooled 'em," said Mister President.

"Thou preparest a table for me in the presence of mine enemies," Chad intoned, and went up his walk to the door.

At Mister President's back door I helped him with the unloading. What, I demanded, was the thing Chad had removed from Gus Blomberg's front yard?

"Well, sir," said Mister President. "It was a device calculated to do the undoable and solve the unsolvable. I couldn't have done better myself."

He sat down on a shell-box on his back steps the better to laugh at his partner's cunning.

[187]

"You know," he said, "when he stuck that thing out there just in the right place, he came back to the blind and told me, 'Mine enemies are lively and they are strong.'"

"What was it?" I insisted. "All I know is there was something out there that made those mallards flare."

Hizzoner picked up the shell-box, his hand on the door knob, and said, "It was Gus Blomberg's scare-crow, and I'm surprised you haven't figgered it out."

"All I could guess was that it was something made of tin cans. I heard 'em rattle."

"Gus Blomberg," said Mister President, "always drapes tin cans on his scarecrows soste they'll rattle in the wind. Good night to you, sir — and don't forget to come over tomorrow night and help me pick these ducks."

Two old soldiers sitting in the kitchen over coffee. Going back into the history of the stream. Giant fish of other days. Other triumphs and a few defeats. Trading and sharing their day and days. Here lie the roots of friendship.

Heartwarming is slowly going extinct. But not in these stories. MacQuarrie constantly throws out little touches that warm one's heart. I'm not going to spoil the next one by telling its secret but the not very surprising ending can only be described as — well, heartwarming. Beneath Mr. President's bluff and bluster, for all his outrageous curmudgeonery, there was something here very warm and winning. Babb of the Brule knew it. MacQuarrie dramatized it.

Babb Of The Brule

"Let us stop and wrap this four-pound rainbow around George's neck," said the President of the Old Duck Hunters' Association with a chuckle.

We were returning from a trout opening on Wisconsin's fabulous and fickle Brule. It was dark and cold. Only the hardiest of the spring peepers sang. The northern lights whirled fluorescent banners. The Old Man got the idea of showing George his big fish while he changed socks in the back seat of the car.

"I'm going to show him this fish."

"Your honor," said I, "Babb will have at least two like it, and his wife will have fifteen, none under a foot."

A wet and sandy wader sock swished alongside my ear. "So you won't stop?"

Very soon we were ascending the front steps of George A. Babb's house.

"It's late, darn near ten-thirty," I whispered.

"Knock!" commanded Hizzoner, both hands around that slab-sided rainbow.

Mrs. Babb opened the door.

"Where's George?"

"George!" Her call went up the stairway.

A sleepy "Who is it?" came down the stairs.

"It's Al," she explained. "He's got a fish he wants to show you."

[192]

"Tell him," said Mister President, "that I want to show him the kind he never catches."

Her voice went dutifully up the stairs again. "He's come to show you up, George, dear."

The bare feet of George A. Babb hit the floor above. Down he came in his night-shirt, tousled and sleepy, but belligerent. There were no formalities between Babb of the Brule and the peerless leader of the Old Duck Hunters. George said, "Produce your minnow."

The rainbow was slid beneath his nose. George took one contemptuous look and headed for the kitchen. He promised en route that presently he would unveil an opening-day catch "fit to take home." He suggested to Mrs. Babb that it was a good time to put on the coffee pot. And he dragged into the living-room, right across the rugs, as mighty an assortment of square-tailed, cold-water fish as this scribe has seen in many a year.

They were in a wash-tub, iced, about two dozen. A few were under a pound. The center of interest was a huge, deep-bellied monster of a rainbow.

"Gargantua!" cried Babb, holding it up alongside Mister President's four-pounder.

"Holy man!" said the President. "It'll go a good five pounds."

"Six and a half!" Babb snorted.

"I guess," said the Old Man, "that I just took in too much territory."

"Like the man who rassled the bear," said George, "you're already yelling 'Stop, or I'll let go!'"

There was vast talk thereafter. George told how he had done it. Salmon eggs and worms with a Colorado spinner early in the day, then big wet flies at midday, and back to bait when the sun rolled under the hill. Mister President managed to issue a few remarks about his own trophy, taken on a black bucktail just below May's Rips. It was a fine meeting until Hizzoner's natural tendencies took charge.

"Tell you what I'll do," he addressed George. "I'll lay you my rod, the one with the 12-inch cork grip, to your waders that next opening night I'll appear on these premises with a bigger rainbow than anything you'll have in that tub."

The hoots of George A. Babb followed us down the steps.

George Babb was perhaps the most proficient fisherman ever to wet a line in the Douglas County Brule. He is the only trout fisherman I know who once announced he would take trout from a certain place, at a certain time, and did it in the presence of a gallery of picnickers.

He came early to the Brule country from Maine. There is a Babb's Island in the Penobscot River of Maine and one in Wisconsin's Flambeau River, both named for logging-day kin of George's. He followed the woods, then took up barbering, fishing and guiding. Although Babb had all the bristly characteristics of a mad porcupine, he had a tender streak in him from here to there. I saw him quit fishing one good evening when accidentally, with a push pole, he knocked a cedar waxwing nest from a tree, drowning the fledgings, while trying to retrieve a hung fly.

He knew the game from A to Z, and loved to disagree with the experts. He had a voice that could boom out a half mile across the Brule's Big Lake. His whisper was a buzz-saw. I am pretty sure that once, for a year or so, he held the world's record for a brown trout, a fish of some 16 pounds, taken about 1916. When a President of the United States came for three months to the Brule, it was Babb who was called on to teach him fly-fishing.

This, then, was Babb, a man who would wrestle you for a dollar and a half any day and give you his last chew of tobacco. Homeward-bound, I reminded Mister President that he was about to lose his pet rod. Soothed by Mrs. Babb's coffee and unruffled about the future, he said: "If there's a fishin' season next year, I'll win."

"Nuts!" said I.

"Wake me up," said he, "when we hit the edge of town. I want to get all my gear in one place so you won't drive off with it."

In the long interim of winter I heard reports of meetings of these two. George would come to town once every so often and stop at Mister President's place of business, mostly to promise Hizzoner that he would have that fly rod, come May First. I heard reports of the two of them locked in mortal combat over fishing tactics, though the thermometer stood at 10 below.

One observer relayed that on a street corner where they met one evening he heard Babb exclaim contemptuously, "That old nine-foot crowbar of yours ain't got but the one tip and that's took a set!"

To which our peerless leader replied, "Your own wife told me you bought those waders the year Taft was elected!"

On opening day I found myself at 4:30 A.M. driving again to the Brule. The Old Man sized up the look of the country as we drove. He said he liked darned near everything that morning. He liked the way the popples were fuzzy when the car lights touched them. He liked the way the season had come belatedly, so that the big migratory rainbows from Lake Superior would still be in the river. He also liked the way the spring peepers were hollering — "like they had a cheer leader."

"But," he continued, "I do not like George A. Babb this morning."

"You're not running out on that bet?"

"Me! I'm just mad at him this morning because I'm sure his darn old waders leak. Ere this day is out his hide will be tacked on the barn door."

I had doubts. Had the field of honor been any of a dozen other north Wisconsin streams, I'd have felt safer about Mister President's rod. Babb knew that Brule like the mink that live along its banks.

There was another reason for concern on my part. Mister President, not at all like himself, didn't know exactly where he wanted to put into the stream. It was not time for confusion. The omens were bad. In fettle, the Old Man would have gone to his chosen place as the bee to the honey tree. He speculated as we drove along.

"I'd hit for the Cloquet bridge, only it might rain and we'd get stuck on those hills. The meadows north of Brule might be all right, but there'll be too many there. Winnebojou is a good starter, but since they tore out the South Shore trestle I don't like the look of it...."

It was breaking day. A decision was in order. No inspired directions came from Mister President; so I nudged his ancient car beyond Winnebojou and down a two-rut road. It's a good place if you get to the end of it with auto springs intact.

He took a long time to get into his waders. He dallied over his gear. He let the leader and line slip back through the guides several times before he had it threaded properly. He asserted that the canned salmon eggs you get nowadays are no good. He exhibited all the insecurity of a lamb getting fat in a feeding pen and not liking it a little bit. It was light when we hit the river.

"I suppose," said Mister President, "that by this time his wife has caught all the trout he needs."

"Who needs?"

"George A. Babb, you derned fool!"

He left me there, preoccupied and, I think, skeptical of this day's luck. I hardly knew whether to laugh or suggest extenuating circumstances, such as substituting another rod for the nonpareil nine-footer. I knew, as

Mister President vanished downstream, that up the river some distance the wizard, Babb, was working a magic line over excellent trout water.

True, Mister President might hang a hook in the mouth of a monster. And George might meet up with a bad day. It was unlikely, though.

The only warm praise I can speak for that cold morning is that there were no mosquitoes. Back from the river bank in the little hollows there was crisp ice. My wader boots crunched through plenty of it as I went upstream along the bank.

The river does a good bit of twisting here. In a few places it has tried to cut cross lots. These are hard to get around, harder to wade through. The business of lifting first one foot and then the other from these mucky-bottomed backwaters served to warm me up. I came to a place where the stream is wadable down its center, with a deep long groove of water under the left bank. Willows tip over it. Perhaps there was something in there.

The routine was followed in the strict early-season tradition for these waters — worms and salmon eggs with spinners and without, then big gaudy flies, then those black bucktails. After four hours all I had was an empty tobacco can which had housed some splendid worms. The river seemed dead. I grew tired of a fruitless campaign beneath the willows, went ashore, lit a fire and stretched.

The sun climbed. The grass beneath me warmed up. I dozed a bit. Then I was suddenly awake, wide awake, for a man was standing over me, tickling my nose with the slightly dried tail of a six-pound rainbow trout. the man was the President of the Old Duck Hunters.

"I've got him!" he exulted. "His waders are practically hanging in my garage this minute. That big one he had last spring was a fluke."

He related that he had found a hole "and stuck with it." He saw the big one roll and worked on him for two hours — "threw a hardward store at him. Finally I dug around and brought up this little wooden wabbler. Bet I showed it to him two hundred times before he took it."

"And when he took it?"

"Then I says, says I, 'George, if those waders leak, you'll have to pay for the vulcanizing!'"

Mister President was indeed jubilant. The contrast with his mood of early morning was impressive. He said he felt so darned good that he would climb the steep hill to the car and bring down a frying-pan — "so I can fry up the little ones you got."

I explained I did not have even one little one, that we did not have a frying-pan in the car, and that he was just trying to rub it in.

"Uh-huh," he said. "Got you both licked." Then he rolled over and fell asleep in the sun.

While he sought that repose to which he was entitled I tried again along this favorite water of mine. The warmer weather helped. We flies attracted interest. I nailed a few — "half a hatful," Mister President said later. "Ain't you ever goin' to catch a fish too big for a creel?"

In the evening we went up the hill out of the steep valley. He sat on the running-board and I pulled off his waders, a ceremony which concludes with the puller being shoved sprawling by the pullee. He permitted me to take down his rod — "and don't leave any rag-tag bobtail of leader wound around the reel."

I cramped the car wheels to get it out of the narrow turn-around, and we started down the two-rut road. Mister President leaned back with the taste of victory in his mouth and chortled, "Wait till you see Babb's face fall."

All the way the Old Man was drinking hot blood, right out of the neck.

"Oh," he said generously, "Babb isn't such a bad fisherman. He'll have some fair fish under the kitchen sink in that dingdanged wash-tub. He'll be in bed when we get there pretending he's asleep and hoping we won't have the heart to bother him. Can't you push this old hack a bit faster?"

He lifted up his voice in snatches of song. One ballad dealt with how tall the chickens grew in Cheyenne. He also gave a sincere rendition of "The Stars and Stripes Forever," but it seemed to me he put his whole best into "The March of the Cameron Men."

Going up the Babb front steps, he was toting that dangling rainbow and humming, "She'll be Comin 'Round the Mountain When She Comes." Babb himself opened the door. Mister President got right down to the bricks immediately. "Bring on your fish!" he demanded.

Babb grinned. You knew when you saw his grin that it was an emblem of defeat. He slapped the Old Man on the back and roared: "You've got me this time, cold turkey. I never saw sign of a fish half that big."

"Bring on the waders!" demanded Mister President.

"Put on the coffee," said George.

There was vast talk thereafter. George told how he had done it — salmon eggs and worms with a Colorado spinner early in the day, then big wet flies at midday, and back to bait when the sun rolled under the hill. Mister President managed to issue a few remarks about his own trophy.

The pair of them, well along, gray and grizzled, did a lot of remembering. They went over the history of the Brule from the 90's and the history of Lake Nebagamon from the days when the Weyerhaeusers had their headquarters there. It was late when we left. Babb brought out the waders, still very damp.

"Looks to me like the darned things leak," Mister President sniffed.

"I'll say they do. I gave them a month's wear just today."

"W-e-l-l," said Mister President in a burst of magnanimity, "what do I want with leaky waders? I just wanted to show you, dang you!"

"That you did," Babb admitted.

Mister President went out the door toward the car. I remained behind, for Babb had plucked my coat sleeve. He whisked me quickly to the kitchen. There was the familiar wash-tub, iced. On top of a welter of trout lay a rainbow — such a trout as men dream of — huge, glistening carmine and olive.

"It's nice of you, George." I said before hurrying out to the car. "You know he's getting old."

"Sure, sure," he said. "I am, too."